The Caring Family

LIVING WITH CHRONIC MENTAL ILLNESS

The Caring Family

LIVING WITH CHRONIC MENTAL ILLNESS

KAYLA F. BERNHEIM,
RICHARD R. J. LEWINE,
CAROLINE T. BEALE

Contemporary Books, Inc.
Chicago

Library of Congress Cataloging in Publication Data

Bernheim, Kayla F.
    The caring family.

    Includes index.
    1. Mentally ill—Home care.   I. Lewine, Richard R. J.
II. Beale, Caroline T.   III. Title.   [DNLM: 1. Mental
disorders—Popular works.   2. Family.   3. Attitude to
health.   WM 100 B527c]
RC439.5.B47   1983   649.8   83-14384
ISBN 0-8092-5534-0

Published by Contemporary Books, Inc.
180 North Michigan Avenue, Chicago, Illinois 60601
Manufactured in the United States of America
International Standard Book Number: 0-8092-5534-0

Published simultaneously in Canada by Beaverbooks, Ltd.
195 Allstate Parkway, Valleywood Business Park
Markham, Ontario L3R 4T8 Canada

Published by arrangement with Random House, Inc.

Foreword

Approximately one out of every ten individuals is at least partially disabled by chronic mental illness.[1] Of the many patients discharged from psychiatric hospitals each year, some 55–70 percent return to live with their families. For many others, families assume a major caretaking role, even when the ill relative lives outside the home. Regardless of the specific form of mental disability or the particular living arrangement, families have come to bear a heavy burden.

Perhaps you are not sure if your relative suffers from a

[1]Schizophrenia, manic-depressive illness, alcohol or drug abuse, severe anxiety, and brain disease or accidents can all lead to chronic mental illness. Extended discussions about each of these disorders are beyond the scope of this book. Interested readers can refer to the glossary and to Kayla F. Bernheim and Richard R. J. Lewine, *Schizophrenia: Symptoms, Causes, Treatments* (New York: W. W. Norton, 1979); Nathan S. Kline, *From Sad to Glad: Kline on Depression* (New York: Simon & Schuster, 1968); and Clara Claiborne Park and Leon N. Shapiro, *You Are Not Alone* (Boston: Little, Brown, 1976).

chronic mental illness. The answer may be yes if your relative has the following characteristics:

High vulnerability to stress. People with chronic mental illness tend to become severely disorganized or symptomatic when confronted with stresses and strains that most people would find pretty easy to handle.

Difficulty in managing daily life. These people often lack or fail to use such basic skills as taking care of personal hygiene, budgeting money, cooking meals, using public transportation, or holding a job.

Extreme dependency. They often feel quite helpless and depend on family or social institutions for a great deal of support. They may become seriously agitated or symptomatic when this support is threatened or withdrawn.

Relationship problems. Chronic mental illness almost always interferes with the ability to maintain close, mutually satisfying relationships with other people.[2]

The Caring Family has been written for all those families having relatives with emotional problems so severe or persistent that they require special support. We hope to reduce some of the secrecy, mystery, and fear surrounding mental illness and, by so doing, to ease the family's burden.

For many years, the mentally ill were routinely shut away in institutions. Ineffective treatments and an "out-of-sight, out-of-mind" attitude of society made return to the community difficult if not impossible, except for those whose symptoms had disappeared entirely. Families of the mentally ill, feeling ashamed and guilty, sought and received little support from professionals, government, or friends. The medical model of treatment fostered a narrow, patient-oriented approach in which the impact on families was underemphasized. Busy men-

[2]Test, Mary Ann and Stein, Leonard L. "Community treatment of the chronic patient: research overview." *Schizophrenia Bulletin,* 1978, *4,* 350–362.

tal health professionals worked hard at trying to cure the patient, but often neglected the needs of the family.

Much of this has changed. Today, more effective treatments have drastically reduced the need for lifetime institutionalization. At the same time, a somewhat more enlightened society is beginning to provide the kinds of social and financial support necessary for community care of the mentally ill. Patients, ex-patients, and their families are becoming more visible and more assertive about their rights and their needs. While all of this will likely lead to a more satisfying and productive life for mentally ill persons in the future, at present many families experience an increasingly severe burden. They are caring for their impaired relatives in the community with, as yet, insufficient information, guidance, and emotional support.

In *The Caring Family* you will find a discussion of the common emotions family members have, including guilt, shame, fear, anger, and despair. Knowing that others experience these feelings too may help you feel less alone. You will find advice about how to handle various problem behaviors that your relative presents, as well as suggestions on how to minimize stress within yourself and within the family. We hope these will increase your comfort and self-confidence. You will find a description of the mental health system and of the legal issues in which families may become enmeshed. Struggling with problems—such as involuntary commitment, the right to refuse treatment, and trust funds to protect your relative after you die—may become somewhat easier as a result. Finally, you will find many excerpts from interviews with other people like you. Their descriptions of the problems they have faced and the various solutions they have developed will, we hope, be both instructive and supportive.

Our indebtedness begins with these family members, who have patiently helped us understand what they have gone through and who have allowed use of quoted material. We must acknowledge their participation anonymously due to the

FOREWORD

still considerable stigma associated with mental illness. To Otto Wahl, Agnes Hatfield, and members of *Threshold* who reviewed and commented on the manuscript, we owe additional thanks. We gratefully acknowledge the contributions of Deborah Holden and Mary Krane. We are grateful as well for the encouragement and assistance of Random House editor Gail Winston, the help of Sharon Medlock, Marsha Healy, and Phyllis Jones in the preparation of the book, and for the critical comments and forbearance of our spouses, Joseph, Janice, and Robert. Any errors or biases remaining are strictly our own.

KFB
RJL
CTB
November 1980

Contents

I

AN OVERVIEW

1

One Family's Story

Tom and Betty Lacey* are a middle-aged, middle-class couple. They own a home in a residential neighborhood in a middle-sized East Coast city. Both come from tight-knit ethnic families. Their brothers, sisters, and cousins are among their best friends.

Tom has worked as a machinist at the same company for twenty-five years. His work, highly respected, earned him a recent promotion. While basically shy and unassuming, Tom has numerous buddies at work with whom he bowls in winter and plays softball in summer. Like many men, he finds talking about his feelings difficult. His affection for his wife is expressed by tousling her hair or teasing her. When he is sad or upset, he retreats to his workshop alone. He is a big bear of a man, usually gentle and quiet, but capable of instilling fear when he gets angry.

*Due to the considerable stigma still associated with mental illness, every attempt has been made to protect the true identity of this family. In all other respects, their story is told as it happened, often in their own words.

3

In contrast, Betty is a small, perky lady. She talks quickly and often. She giggles readily and cries when she needs to. She is working now as a receptionist, but has spent most of the last twenty years as a housewife, caring for her family and her home.

The Laceys are like millions of other American families except in one respect: They have a mentally ill son. Having such a son has radically changed the direction of their lives. In this chapter we hope to use the Laceys' experiences to highlight the feelings, concerns, and problems shared by all families with a mentally ill member.

Steve Lacey was born when his sister, Sarah, was four years old. His mother describes the labor as a difficult one that produced a small but apparently normal baby. Although he was quiet as an infant, Steve became overly active and hard to control as a young child. When he was five years old he could not sit still long enough for Betty to read him a story, and he seemed unable to follow even simple instructions. The "terrible twos" seemed to drag on and on. Steve's temper tantrums, which could occur anyplace at any time, made social outings unpleasant. But the problem that most worried Tom and Betty was that Steve was able to speak no more than a few words by the time he started kindergarten.

The next ten years were spent with speech therapists, physicians, teachers, and social workers, each of whom offered a different explanation and different advice. One predicted that Steve would never have serious problems because he was so outgoing. She told the Laceys that quiet, conscientious Sarah was more at risk for emotional problems. Another told them that Steve was brain-damaged, while yet another said that he couldn't be because he was too alert: "His eyes are too alive." Whereas a physician prescribed medication for Steve's "hyperactive" behavior, a school social worker told the family to exert more discipline but did not help them learn how to do that.

4

Lack of support from the school, the church, even the family, made matters worse for the Laceys. At school the teachers complained that Steve was disruptive. He asked too many questions and made too much noise. They were reluctant to give Steve the extra attention his parents thought he needed. Nor were they helpful with Steve's medication regimen.

> BETTY: I got a little upset with the teachers. I wanted to bring the medicine there and leave it in the nurse's office or with the principal. I didn't want him carrying it. I didn't want the other children getting it. And the teachers wouldn't do it. I finally had to beg her [the teacher] to at least watch him, to see that he would take it himself. I wouldn't want him to throw it out. I felt very bad about that.

School officials seemed insensitive to the family's feelings as well as to Steve's needs.

> BETTY: In the eighth or seventh grade, the principal came to the store where I worked. Luckily I wasn't cashing. I still don't forgive her for that. She could have called me at home. She didn't have to embarrass me! She told me that I should do something about Stevie.

At church the same sort of thing occurred.

> TOM: He was an altar boy, too. No one except Stevie would get up to serve the early mass. Well, he quit. Then something came up and they needed someone to volunteer to help serve. Stevie volunteered, but Monsignor said, "No, you quit." That made me very angry. The kid was willing to give it a try. They knew he was having problems. It was something good that he wanted to do, and they refused him.

Worst of all, the Laceys' relatives had decided that Steve was just a bad kid, and they let Tom and Betty know it.

TOM: My father always told me that Stevie would be trouble because Stevie wouldn't listen.

BETTY: I used to get provoked at his father because he would say things about Stevie being a baby, you know. My mother too. Sarah was without sin. No one could say anything bad about Sarah. Even if they didn't say anything, you could feel it. And it would bother me, too, because I thought that that didn't help. It seemed like everybody was telling him, "Well, you're naughty. You're bad."

Tom and Betty could not accept the judgment that Steve was just a naughty child. Often he did household chores without being asked, and he readily shared his toys with other children. He loved hugging and delighted in making people laugh. Tom and Betty hated to see Steve's quick tears brought on more and more frequently by harsh words and stern looks. They felt they had to make up to Steve for the lack of affection he received from others. At the same time, his behavior could be so frustrating, so uncontrollable! Little by little, the Laceys began to accommodate themselves to the situation. Each attempted to reduce the level of disruption and guilt, to make minute-by-minute living a little more tolerable.

Betty felt a special need to protect her son and was constantly torn between her attention to Steve and to other members of her family.

BETTY: Stevie always had problems. That's why I catered to him so much. And then again, too, I didn't help him too much because I learned all his motions. You know, every time he wanted something, I knew what he wanted and I would give it to him. It seemed like such an effort for him to have to ask me when I knew. And maybe that kind of slowed him down a little bit.

I remember my cousin started to laugh at me once. We were trying to have coffee, and I was taking things from Stevie's reach and putting them on the refrigerator. And I didn't realize I was doing this. I was doing it automatically.

It's easier to give in to him. You're there and it's not just you that's being affected by it—my husband is there too. If we start yelling, that upsets him, you know. So I have to consider Steve—that he's sick. It's a lousy merry-go-round!

Betty recalls feeling almost all of the time that whatever she did was wrong. And no wonder, given the balancing act she was trying to perform. She tried to give Steve consistent discipline while shielding him from the critical judgments of others. She tried to attend to Sarah's needs in spite of Steve's incessant demands on her time. She tried to be a wife to Tom, although her energy was always drained. Unable to be everything to everyone, Betty felt constantly guilty and incompetent. Nobody ever seemed satisfied, including Betty.

Meanwhile, Tom was struggling with many conflicting feelings. He was intensely disappointed in his only son. He had envisioned a son he could be proud of, a son who would be good at sports, personable, and clever. Instead, he felt embarrassed when Steve accompanied him to baseball games or bowling matches. During these outings, Steve constantly disrupted the adults' activities. If he was not asking somebody for a candy bar, he was interrupting somebody else's conversation. When the adults taught the children how to play, Steve could not seem to learn. He could not even pay attention. The worst part was that he completely ignored Tom's attempts to control or discipline him.

It was hard for Tom to play with Steve even though he knew he should. In fact, it was even hard to like this child who was so loud, disruptive, and demanding. Tom found himself angry at Steve almost all of the time they were together. Tom would too often lose his temper and yell. This seemed to upset Betty and did not do any good anyway. He did not know how to talk about his feelings, and besides, he did not want to burden Betty even more. He could not seem to help. In confusion and frustration, he began to spend more and more time alone. From Tom's perspective, leaving Betty in charge was best for everybody. Nonetheless, Tom often felt guilty about his withdrawal from Steve and tried to compensate by giving in to his son's constant demands.

> TOM: I used to try to please him most of the time. He always wanted to go swimming. We'd come back at one o'clock. He'd want to go back [to the pool] at three. I used to take him.

Steve's need for almost constant attention had taken its toll on his sister, Sarah. From the beginning she had been a placid, agreeable child who demanded little. She rarely showed anger. Her unhappiness was more readily expressed as sadness and withdrawal. As she grew up, she became a good student, and although she had friends, she seemed content to spend much of her time on schoolwork or reading.

At times Sarah wished that Steve had never been born. No matter how hard she tried, no matter how good she was, she could not seem to get her parents' attention. Steve seemed to pursue her relentlessly, breaking her toys, pulling her hair, acting up in front of her friends. He would always apologize after one of these episodes. Seemingly contrite, he promised to be good, only to break that promise within a short time. It appeared to her that he could get away with anything. Anger at her brother and at her parents warred with guilt and the fervent wish for demonstrations of their love.

In spite of the love that Tom and Betty had for each other and for their two children, there was frequent and painful conflict at home. Betty was often angry with Tom for leaving her so much in charge.

> BETTY: Well, I think when things didn't go right, it was my fault. Everything was thrown on me, "do what you think is best." But then when things didn't turn out right—well, then, "Why did you do it this way?" And that would bother me. It still does.

Nor did Tom seem very eager to hear about the day-to-day problems she had. The more she tried to talk to him, the more he withdrew. Sometimes it seemed to her that Tom did not care about his son at all.

Often Tom was not pleased with Betty's way of disciplining Steve. She protected him too much and lectured him instead of making him mind. Tom felt that Steve would respond better to a firm, clear approach, but when he tried to put his foot down, Betty would turn on him, crying that Stevie could not help the way he was.

Each was aware that the other usually thought there was a "better" way to handle each incident. Each felt unsupported by the other and guilty about being short-tempered with the other. The level of tension between them was high.

Yet they never let a dispute last very long. Neither of them was afraid to be the first to "give in." A hug from Tom or a freshly baked apple pie from Betty usually made things right again.

They deeply regretted their lack of opportunity to relax and enjoy each other. Steve was far too difficult to leave with a baby-sitter, so they did not go out much.

BETTY: Sarah and my nephew Sammy would take turns staying at my mother's house. Stevie couldn't understand why he wasn't wanted there. But they just couldn't cope with him. He was too active.

The Laceys began making excuses for not attending family gatherings, because they were sure to be embarrassed by Steve's behavior. They did not invite friends over very often, either, for the same reason. Gradually, their social circle became smaller and smaller.

Sarah felt overwhelmed by the tension and confusion in the household. Despite her best intentions she squabbled with Steve more than she felt she should. She hated to see her parents argue and found herself taking sides, trying to settle the disagreement. While this always seemed to make the situation worse, she could not just stand by helplessly.

As a teen-ager, Sarah began to spend more and more time away from home. She involved herself in many school activities and went to the homes of her friends, rarely inviting anybody to her home. Her parents tacitly supported this strategy, since they could not seem to prevent the almost constant battling between their two children. They admitted, though with guilt, that things seemed much more peaceful when Sarah was gone.

Steve felt the tension too. His parents' arguments confused and agitated him. He knew he was somehow at fault, but he was not sure what everybody wanted from him. His mother tolerated behavior that his father punished him for, and Sarah seemed never to want him around at all. Afraid and insecure, he continued to seek reassurance and attention in any way he could.

Nonetheless, Steve's early school years had their rewarding moments. In those years Steve made many friends, played softball, participated in the soapbox derby, and joined in church activities. His parents remember with greatest pleasure his success with a paper route as a fifth- and sixth-grader.

Ironically, the paper route may have contributed indirectly to Steve's emerging mental illness.

> TOM: The problem really started when he was between thirteen and fourteen. He started to make money from the paper route, and I think he started to buy drugs.

With increasing drug use, Steve became more and more erratic. During one of their now frequent arguments, Steve lost his temper and threw a pitchfork at his father. Badly frightened, Betty insisted that Steve be eveluted at the local mental health center. However, Steve ran away to another city before that evaluation could be completed.

BETTY: He would call us, but he would never tell us where he was. Finally, one evening we got a call that Stevie was in jail. They caught him with some marijuana, and we had to pick him up. I was so nervous. I had never been in a courtroom before. I even forgot his birthdate!

The Laceys were able to convince the judge to release Steve on probation. They were doing their best to get help for Steve, and he was scheduled to enter high school in a few days. When they returned home, frightened and in need of support, the Laceys appealed to the local family court for help in keeping Steve in treatment and enforcing rules at home. They were turned down by a judge who told them that Steve did not need psychiatric care, they did.

Steve's behavior got progressively worse once he started high school. He found his attention wandering and his ability to concentrate on his studies dwindling. His grades began to drop and he felt like a failure. At the same time his moodiness and unpredictability drove away his friends. He felt hurt and angry that he was no longer invited to parties or other social events. His isolation was compounded by his own feelings that somehow he was changing, becoming different from everyone else. Refusing to stay in class, he wandered the halls, disrupting other classes. While still on probation, Steve was caught with drugs. Betty describes the events following his second arrest:

BETTY: He ran out of the courtroom, I remember. I got scared! You just don't run out of a courtroom. The judge stopped everything. She was such a nice person. She explained to me that that's what happens when they take drugs. She said, "Don't feel badly. He's not the first one." Instead of taking him back to detention, she sent him to Community Hospital. This was the first time he was ever in the hospital and the first time he was ever on Thorazine.

11

TOM: This was all new to us. When the doctor said he had to stay four or five days, I thought that was a long time, but I thought he'd be all healed up—you know, that he'd be a new man or something, a new kid.

The Laceys' hopes for a miracle cure were soon dashed. Once out of the hospital, Steve returned to heavy drug use. His behavior at home was becoming nearly intolerable. He teased and taunted his sister until she cried. He threatened and cursed his mother when he was not begging a favor or apologizing for something in the past. He began pushing and punching Betty when he did not get his way. Rather than tell Tom about this and risk a violent confrontation, Betty began to hide the bruises and lie about how she had gotten them. Tom, also apprehensive about a catastrophic battle with his son, appeared not to notice the increasingly frequent welts on her upper arms. Unable to think of any alternatives, Betty and Tom gave in more and more to Steve's demands until he ruled the household in a reign of terror.

Steve's behavior was becoming bizarre and extremely demanding. He spent a great deal of time alone listening to rock-and-roll at a volume that shook the walls. He spent hours in the shower, sometimes taking four long showers a day. He became interested in witchcraft and began to talk about the devil and to accuse his mother of being a witch. Finally, shortly before his fifteenth birthday, Steve completely lost touch with reality. On a day when Betty had gone to a neighboring city to visit family, Steve became agitated and ordered Tom to take a shower to "clean out the spirits." Tom came out of the bathroom just in time to see Steve run naked into the backyard. As his father watched, Steve dug a hole, buried a book in it, and jumped the fence into a neighbor's yard. Before Tom could think what to do next, Steve ran in the front door and ordered his father to remove his gold wedding band and get back in the shower. Steve was holding a large rock, and his wild expression convinced Tom not to argue.

TOM: He was so paranoid. That was the first episode in which we were really scared. He was so paranoid that his mother had left him alone for the day, and I guess he couldn't handle it.

Steve eventually calmed down, but this episode convinced Tom and Betty that he needed more help.

Betty tried to have Steve admitted to several inpatient units. One had no beds available. One had no facilities for young people. One would not take any violent patients. Heartsick, she gave up. Upon the advice of their local mental health center, the Laceys took Steve to the state mental hospital.

BETTY: They said that it would take a while, but that he could be helped. They recommended going to the state. They said they had a special unit there just for kids, set aside from the other units.

TOM: I remember Sarah putting up such a ruckus: "How could you leave your son in that place?" She was in high school then. I was really torn. I didn't know if I was doing right or wrong. I felt guilty. When Sarah got through with me, I thought, "My God, I can't do this to my son! I want to help him, but I don't know what to do."

BETTY: I agreed to it because I couldn't keep him at home the way he was. I had no choice.

Over the next eight years, Steve was in and out of the hospital many times. Tom estimates that Steve spent three and a half of those years in the institution.

TOM: There were times I couldn't go up there anymore. I thought he'd never snap out of it. I used to stay in the car in the parking lot. Betty would go up there and he used to try to hit her, spit in her face. It was really heavy. It was really, really bad. When we had to move him from hospital to hospital, we had to have an ambulance, have him tied down, handcuffed!

Steve ran away from the hospital more than once. He was terrified of the locked doors and the other patients. He felt abandoned by his parents and angry that they had put him in such a place. Most of all he felt that he did not need to be there. He felt that he needed only more understanding and affection. At home between hospitalizations, Steve's behavior was unimproved.

BETTY: I couldn't even go down to the cellar without him following me. And oh, how he teased Sarah! He could make her cry just by looking at her. We felt terrible about that, about how he treated her. But we just didn't know how to handle it. We were all so on edge. He got progressively worse. He would turn on me for just anything. He would slap me. He would push me, and naturally I would go flying. Sometimes I'd hit my head. But then he'd say he was sorry.

One night my husband was outside cutting the grass, and Steve was blasting his record player, and I was trying to do the dishes. I said, "Please, Stevie, lower that," and he got mad and with his foot he kicked me! And I said, "Oh no, I can't put up with this. He's got to go back to the hospital."

TOM: I've been hit [by Steve] over the head with a telephone. One time he got my glasses—he pulled them off my face and just broke them in half. And doors were broken down. We had a lot of help with cops.

BETTY: It was terrible because they had to put him in a strait jacket sometimes.

TOM: Remember the doctors—him spitting right in their faces? It was really, really rough.

Despite his aggressive, demanding, and socially inept behavior, Steve was at least somewhat able to look after himself. Two years ago, at the urging of professionals who were concerned about the deteriorated quality of the Laceys' home life, Tom and Betty helped Steve move into his own apartment. He was twenty-one years old. At first he refused to go, accusing his parents of not loving him and threatening bodily harm if they attempted to force him. Finally, in the face of their firm insistence, he changed his mind.

While Tom and Betty regained at least partial control of their home, their responsibility for Steve was far from over. At the time of this writing, Betty does his laundry, cleans his apartment, handles his money, and buys his food and clothing. Tom acts as chauffeur and delivery boy. Often Steve calls three or more times an evening or appears at the house to take a shower, listen to the radio, or raid the refrigerator. The Laceys continually run interference for Steve with landlords, neighbors, friends, and acquaintances. Despite their efforts, they have had to move him four times in two years.

TOM: Four places. That's not bad in two years. Four places. The first one he got thrown out the first month. The next one he lasted a whole year because I got a couple of friends in there and they covered up for him. It was simple things he just couldn't do. You can't go barging in doors without knocking —things like that.

In this last place I knew Stevie was in the clear because the super stopped me and we talked for about twenty minutes. He was telling me that Stevie was making eyes at his wife and talking to her, and he said, "I watched him for a couple of days and I knew the kid was more or less harmless." I mean, he understood Stevie and he told me he'd try to talk to some of the tenants and keep an eye on Stevie and help him out.

BETTY: He wants to make friends. He's really harmless, but you can't start knocking on everybody's door. I mean, people want privacy. He made a nuisance out of himself, so the first night I got a call. Another time, he played his record player loud and the lady downstairs complained about it. Once he called the police twice in one night to complain because an acquaintance hadn't returned his bicycle.

Keeping Steve in an apartment is not the Laceys' only worry. Sarah, bitter about the chaos Steve's behavior has brought to their lives and resentful about the years of attention lavished on her brother, has decided to see Steve as little as possible.

> SARAH: It's not that I don't love him. I just can't stand watching what he does to them. He does things just to get to them ... I don't know, maybe he can't help it, but I just can't stand to watch it anymore. When he's there, I get mad at him, at them. It's just awful.

She wants to see her parents, though, and again Betty feels caught in the middle:

> Right now Sarah's very blue. She's so concerned about the holidays, you know. She's got her in-laws. She's got her husband with her. She's not alone. And she says, "Aren't you coming over at all on Christmas?" And I say, "You know my hands are tied. I can't come over Christmas if Stevie's home." It isn't fair.
> It just isn't fair that I should leave Stevie to go over there. I said, "My door is open. If you want to come over here, you can. I'm not going to leave your brother alone." Because she's not alone, you know. She says, "No, it would be too much. The tension would be too much, with Stevie and all, especially now that he's not taking his medicine."

But Sarah says, "I just wanted them to come for Christmas Eve. Is that too much to ask? After all, they're my parents too." Tom has trouble understanding Sarah's attitude:

> It really hurts. I think Sarah could help him out, understand that he's sick. But I'm a different person. Her feelings are the way they are.
> It's her life and she's got a right to feel the way she wants to feel. And, too, Stevie has sort of robbed her of a lot of our attention. This is the way she sees it.

But like I said, Stevie's the one leading a dog's life. He's alone all the time. Nobody wants him.

All the while in the back of everyone's mind lingers the fear that Steve will get worse again and will have to be rehospitalized, beginning the whole cycle anew. The Laceys have ample reason to be concerned. Eight months ago Steve stopped taking his medication. A few weeks later he began to believe that people were trying to poison him.

> BETTY: For some reason or other he must have really flipped. He had thrown everything away. There was no food in the apartment at all. He'd taken all the dishes out of the pantry and put them in the sink. He threw away his keys . . . and I found his pants on a tree limb, outside the apartment!

During the six weeks that Steve was in the hospital and not receiving Social Security disability checks, Tom and Betty paid his rent and fed his cat every day. It was easier than finding him a new place when he got out.

At present Steve is again threatening to stop taking his medicine. By law he cannot be forced to take it.

> BETTY: I don't think they have the right to make that decision. I really don't. If a person is sound of mind and doesn't want to take any medicine, doesn't want to prolong his life, and he knows what he's talking about, I can understand that. But in Stevie's case he doesn't know the seriousness of it. He's only hurting himself, and hurting the people around him, and causing misery all the way around.
>
> I finally said to him, "Don't tell me about it, that's all." I mean, here I am at work doing the daily report, and I'm thinking about my son going berserk again . . .

The Laceys feel very much alone in coping with their problems. They are bitter that other relatives have not taken their

17

share of the responsibility. Their few friends, unsure of how to help, avoid the subject altogether.

> TOM: People could have done more—a little comfort or sympathy, or even if they were fooling us, respect him a little more. I'm speaking of good friends, my brother, Betty's brother. They could ask, "How's Stevie doing?" or "Is it possible for me to go see him?" once in a blue moon or "Can I send him a card?" He never got a card from anybody. It's like he didn't exist.

> BETTY: I remember once telling my sister-in-law the same thing. I said, "Martha, if Stevie had broken his leg, you'd be on the phone asking." I think people don't ask because they think they're going to hurt you by asking. So they pretend that it doesn't exist. But it does exist. You love that person. He is sick. He hasn't got control over it. He's sick and he's part of you. People think it's something to be really ashamed of. But my son didn't want this illness any more than he'd want a broken leg.
>
> You know, people look at him and physically he looks great. They'll carry on that he's lazy or this or that. They just don't understand.

How are Tom and Betty feeling about their lives at this point? They have more realistic expectations now. No longer hoping for complete recovery, they are grateful for small improvements. They point out that Steve is less aggressive now, that he doesn't seem to be taking street drugs, that he keeps his apartment fairly neat. But they're getting weary.

> TOM: We haven't given up yet, I'll tell you that. He's still got time—he's only twenty-three. But I've always got that fear, you know, that something terrible will happen. The other day we got a phone call at five-thirty in the morning. We thought it was Stevie. It wasn't. We always figure it's going to be Stevie.
>
> Truthfully, what we've gone through, it's tougher now. It's

bothering me more now. When he comes to the house and he wants to have lunch or take a shower, I still do the same old thing. I go to my workshop. Why should I take a chance of getting angry? I still run from the possibility. And Betty, she's very high-strung. She's yelling quite a bit and she never used to yell—I mean, not just with Stevie, but with me, with her mother. She's got Stevie branded on her mind.

BETTY: It's not good because it's very hard on me. Whenever anything happens, "Call Betty Lacey," or "Betty, you take care of it." You know, I'm getting to the point where I don't really want to be bothered. I'm not at peace with myself. I want to give him more independence, but I can't say, "To hell with you." I just can't say that. I feel bad for Stevie because he's the one who's missed out on life, not me.

I get kind of tired. I've been not just seeing professionals, but I've been going back and forth for Stevie. All my life I've been going for Stevie. And Stevie's progressed a little bit, but with all this running around, you'd think he'd have done better.

TOM: You're just driving along and you think, "How's he ever going to make it?" There's no chance in the world that he's going to make it, I think. I really do. No way he's going to make it. It feels very, very depressing.

BETTY: You know, most mothers, they hope their kids go to college. Gee, if he could just make hamburgers, wash dishes, take care of himself. I just want him to have some pride and have something that's his own someday. Just something of his own.

2

Recognizing Mental Illness

Steve Lacey had emotional and behavioral problems for so long that the line between mental health and illness could never be clearly drawn. However, this is not true in all cases. Sometimes a break occurs suddenly and without apparent warning. Sudden and extreme shifts of interest may presage mental disability. A family member, for example, may unexpectedly start talking about plans to save the world; agitated excitement may replace moderate moods; a new hobby that requires long periods alone may suddenly develop. The breaking of many former friend-ships and an intolerance for social interaction can also signal serious disorder.

Far more frequently, however, the change from acceptable behavior to mental illness seems to occur gradually, as it did with Steve. The person may seem just a bit odd at first, a "real character." Then there may be some problems at school or at work, suggesting that all is not well. Nevertheless, everyone has difficult moments, so these early conflicts are usually not seen as serious. Over the months or years, the behavior becomes a bit more bizarre, more abrasive, and less excusable. Then one day, without understanding why or even being aware of when it happened, the family recognizes that the hostility, the eccentricity, and the difficulty are not normal.

Obstacles Against Early Recognition

Mental health professionals do not want to label someone too early. This anti-labeling perspective has emerged from our understanding of the potential harm in the use of diagnostic labels. There can be no doubt that mental disability, in its many forms, and irrespective of the names we attach to them, continues to be a social stigma. Both the public and professionals have stereotyped expectations of the mentally ill that may contribute to a self-fulfilling prophecy. Many ex-patients have described how professional expectations led them to expect so little of themselves and to doubt their ability to ever return to their communities. After all, they reasoned, their doctors told them that they were handicapped, then it must be so. We know, furthermore, that labels can prejudice our way of seeing and interacting with people. Whether that label is a diagnosis, a race, or an ethnic group, it means something to us, which affects our view of the person assigned the label. We are all familiar with common stereotypes: Jews are cheap, Blacks are lazy, and schizophrenics are violent. Such stereotypes are potent and difficult to dispel.

To avoid the possible abuse of diagnostic labels and the social stigma of mental illness, professional judgment often will be withheld. This professional "let's wait and see" attitude, while frequently well-intentioned, serves to delay the family's recognition of mental illness and to produce a feeling of frustration. As many family members have expressed it, "If the professionals can't (or won't) tell you what is happening, who will?"

Another common obstacle to the recognition of mental illness in a family member is the hope that the individual is merely passing through a stage. For example, if a person has been seen as "troublesome" or "willful" in the past, then emerging mental illness may well be viewed as a further extension of this established personality style. Or we may tell ourselves that there is something wrong at work, that all teen-agers go through this, that I have not been thoughtful enough lately.

Adolescent turmoil presents a particular problem for parents of a psychiatrically disturbed child. As children reach sexual maturity, they enter a period of their lives during which they stretch parental limits as far as they can, try new and varied styles, and turn toward rebellious forms of discovering themselves. This sort of adolescent behavior, often seen by parents as a purposeful assault against them, is frequently nothing more than the child's attempt to establish physical, emotional, and psychological independence. Steve Lacey, for example, began to experiment with drugs when he was thirteen or fourteen years old. There are literally thousands of adolescents who take drugs and act strangely, but who never develop a mental illness. Steve Lacey's parents, therefore, were not sure if his difficulties were a result of the drugs or whether Steve's drug use was yet another sign of his mental illness.

An adolescent who eventually does develop serious problems has the same conflicts and the same needs for independence and often engages in the same behavior as his or her peers. Parents are not sure, therefore, whether this adolescent's actions represent expectable rebellion or something more serious. Unfortunately, professional attitudes and advice during this time can harm as much as help.

Finally, there is a common tendency to tolerate or normalize deviant behavior in our own families. Whereas the neighbor's husband may be a "wild man" with a terrible temper and sick attitude toward children, *my* husband just gets frustrated and must "let off steam." The neighbor's child may be "bizarre," whereas mine is "creative." Consider for a moment the last time a non-family member was critical of someone within your immediate family. The inclination is to defend the "attacked" family member and to reduce the magnitude of the critique. Similarly, we tend to reduce the seriousness and importance of deviance in the mentally disabled family member. Tom and Betty Lacey found themselves protecting their son from the criticisms of others. Indeed, they even felt compelled to compensate Steve for the lack of attention and warmth outside the home.

Thus, gradual onset of symptoms, professional reticence about labeling, and families' habitual ways of seeing one another all work against the early recognition of mental illness. As a consequence mental health professionals are sometimes not consulted until a dramatic, occasionally life-threatening event occurs, as it did when Steve Lacey raised the rock over his father's head. The ill person himself may be the target. Sometimes he may have become so confused that simple precautions for safety and personal hygiene are not undertaken. Many families turn to professional help when the ill family member wanders into the street, starts out on long journeys with no planning, or begins to neglect diet, dress, and cleanliness. One seriously disoriented person, for instance, decided on the spur of the moment to take a cross-country trip. He literally got up and left, in the middle of the winter, with no shoes, coat, or money. Another family was finally forced to seek outside help when one spouse threatened another with a knife. Other ill persons may begin to buy extravagantly, give everything away, or make grandiose plans that interfere with normal family functioning. Clearly, when a family member becomes so disturbed that life or health is threatened, the problem can no longer be contained within the family. Few people would disagree about the advisability of seeking professional attention at this point. There is, however, a common and extremely complex bind within which families are placed when a family member may not be quite obviously disturbed enough to be a danger.

One family tells of their son, a young man in his early twenties, who had a violent temper. Though this individual had never directly threatened anyone, his parents were concerned that his bursts of outrage were getting out of hand. On more than one occasion, this family called police and mental health professionals to help them in diffusing their son's rage. The police could do nothing before an actual act had occurred; the mental health professionals were reluctant to undertake outpatient therapy with a young man who had a history of physical violence (such as throwing furniture, breaking down doors). The family—parents and siblings—was left on its own to deal with the increasingly violent son. This particular story does not have a happy ending. Eventually, after the family spent many months unsuccessfully seeking some way to cope with the dilemma, its ill member stabbed a friend to death. The young man is now in a psychiatric hospital for the criminally insane, with only minimal hope for discharge. As the family of this young man asked, "Why did it have to come to this? Why couldn't something have been done *before* the tragic event?"

Unhappily for everyone involved, there are no simple answers to these anguished questions. Our laws are written to protect individuals from the denial of their freedom. As many family members can testify, the emphasis on individual patients' rights seems to interfere with the family's attempts to get help or involve themselves in treatment. It is the nature of many psychiatric disorders that the person affected is unaware of the illness and its effect upon daily life. If a mentally disabled person, therefore, says nothing is wrong, dramatic and convincing evidence is needed to prove otherwise. We cannot hospitalize or jail people because they *might* hurt themselves or others. This is as it should be. However, this knowledge does little to ease the emotional pain or practical difficulties that families face.

Many families find themselves fighting laws and professionals to obtain information and help in caring for the mentally ill. Rather than working together to solve the problems and ease the burden of mental disability, families, patients, and professionals are too often locked into a battle in which everyone emerges a loser.

Accepting the Diagnosis

Emotional responses to mental disability vary considerably at different points in the illness. The family's initial reaction to the behavior of the ill member is untempered by the knowledge that the person is ill. The family's feelings are those that emerge naturally in everyday interactions. If someone yells at you, wrongly accuses you, or disregards your feelings, you may feel hurt or angry. If someone lets you down, fails to do what you expect, you will feel disappointed.

Similarly, an ill relative will anger, disappoint, hurt, or frustrate you. Not having any reason to believe that your child, spouse, sibling, or parent is mentally ill, you will respond as would anyone in such a situation. Therefore, until mental illness is recognized, all family members are subject to these normal responses. Though they will feel guilty in retrospect ("I should have known he wasn't well"), they should be reassured that their emotional reactions were not the cause of the chronic disability.

A next stage for many families is a period of confusion, which arises from the failure of usual explanations to account for the ill member's behavior. If it is not a "phase" or maliciousness or willfulness, then what is going on? When a serious event brings the family to mental health professionals, the answer to this question may come quickly. For those families who have a less dramatically, though equally seriously, disturbed member, the answer may take a long time.

"What is going on?" may be answered in two ways. "Mental disability," "emotional upset," or "nervous breakdown" are all general terms used to explain the disordered behavior. Labels such as "schizophrenia," "manic-depressive psychosis," and "anxiety disorder" are used to describe specific disorders. The family's reaction upon first hearing any of these words may range from shock to relief. In our culture shame and guilt are two of the most frequent feelings expressed by families when they learn of their member's disturbance, since our tradition is to attribute much of the blame of psychological disorder to the family and especially to the parents.

Disbelief is also common. When learning of any potentially serious disorder, the natural tendency is to say, "No, it can't be true, perhaps there has been some mistake." Professionals generally are sensitive to this sort of response when telling patients and families about cancer, multiple sclerosis, epilepsy, and a host of other medical disorders. Patients and families' disbelief in response to clear medical disorders is accepted as natural, as an attempt to reduce the shock. In the case of psychological disorders, however, such normal disbelief frequently is interpreted by professionals as part of the "family pathology." Family members are described as "denying," "resisting," or "sabotaging"; they are not allowed to disbelieve. To find it difficult to accept a diagnosis is a normal response; it need not indicate psychological disorder.

Acceptance of a diagnosis also may wax and wane with the well-being of the ill family member. Some families find it easier to accept mental illness when the relative is acutely ill. When, however, the more dramatic symptoms abate and more subtle difficulties remain, such families may find it hard to accept that the person still is ill. Unlike physical handicaps, mental disability does not have clear visual reminders of the individual's condition. Under these circumstances, families may require several trial-and-error periods to learn the extent of the mental disability.

When the family eventually confronts the fact of mental illness, its members may express anger: "Why should we be picked out?" "Why didn't someone tell us sooner?" "It isn't fair!" All of these reactions occur frequently in other situations, such as in response to suicide or in learning of a serious medical illness. Anger may be directed at the ill person for being sick and creating burdens on the family. Sometimes the anger finds expression in increased irritability and conflict among family members. At other times, family members turn against outsiders—professionals, society, or other families not affected by mental illness.

Finally, families who have traveled these emotional rapids may feel a strong sense of relief. Many family members find it comforting to know what is wrong, to have a name for the disorder, and to have something concrete to tackle. Professionals' reluctance to give labels and to talk about specific problems only further confuses family members who are trying to gain understanding. Part of human nature is to make sense, to provide explanations of the things that go on in our lives. Part of this structuring process requires information about mental illness. Therefore, families should seek as much information as possible from professionals, although this will not always be easy.

Contact with the Mental Health System

Once the family has decided to seek professional help, it faces the practical problem of determining the most appropriate place to go. This period can be a most confusing and frustrating time as people begin to discover the vast array of mental health professionals and facilities available. Sometimes families give up rather than try to sort out the many alternatives. Such a response is not surprising, as there are many professionals who cannot themselves keep track of all the resources.

An excellent starting point for those people with no previous experience with the mental health system is a book by Clara C. Park and Leon N. Shapiro, *You Are Not Alone* (Boston: Little, Brown, 1976). The authors give excellent sketches of the different types of therapy, theories, and professional attitudes families can expect. Financial resources and living facilities are also described. Overall, this book is an invaluable introduction to the mental health maze, its personnel, and its resources.

As a family member, you can expect that involvement in your relative's treatment will be difficult at best. The families of the mentally disabled essentially have no legal rights (unless the ill member is a child under legal age) with respect to records, discharge, or knowledge of the ill person's whereabouts. One mother spent an entire night calling all the local hospitals, outpatient facilities, and emergency rooms trying to locate her son, who had wandered out in the middle of a cold winter night. As it turned out, her son had been admitted to the first hospital she contacted—although she had been told that her son was not there. This sort of professional response to family members is not necessarily malicious. The laws are quite clear in restricting the information that may be given to anyone, including the ill person's family. The result, however, is to force a wedge between many parts of the mental health system and the families of the mentally disabled.

Commitment laws, written to protect the individual, may impede rather than help the families of the mentally ill obtain treatment. Many families must call on police and swear out warrants to have an ill member taken to the hospital. Recall that this is only after some serious event, such as an act of violence, has taken place. The consequences of being forced to use such measures to ensure that a loved one is seen in treatment are devastating. Family members feel guilty and ashamed; they are angry at the law and the mental health profession that forces them to take these sorts of actions; they fear how the ill family member will respond. To be the recipient of such treatment is no better. The ill family member may feel betrayed, like a criminal, confused, angry, frightened, or more likely some combination of all of these. The shock families feel and the personal conflict caused by the legal restrictions cannot be imagined in advance.

Another hurdle facing those families who want a collaborative relationship with the mental health professionals is traditional psychological theory. Since it is common for professionals to view family members, especially parents, as playing a major role in the development of mental disorder, families of the mentally disabled are seen as candidates for therapy rather than as partners in caring for the ill person. If the mental health professional first contacted by the family has such views, then the family's attempts to seek help may be rebuffed or family therapy suggested.

It may be difficult to locate a professional willing to accept a patient with a history of violence or suicide attempts. One young woman who was seriously considering suicide went through a half-dozen names in the yellow pages before finding someone who would see her. When there is a serious threat to life involved in the mental disability, more success is likely to be had with clinics and hospitals than with private practitioners. Such professional behavior can transmit two messages to disturbed persons and their families: A rebuff may be taken as evidence that the problems are either too difficult to handle or of no importance. Naturally after such an experience families may feel that their situation is hopeless. Nevertheless, through trial and error, sometimes through the guidance of local clinics, hospitals, or families' groups, many families do eventually locate a sympathetic resource person. But perhaps the most difficult lesson to be learned by families of the chronically mentally disabled is that treatment does not guarantee success. Remember Tom's hopes about his son's first hospitalization: "I thought he'd be all healed up—you know, that he'd be a new man or something, a new kid." Such hopes are fantasies for families of the chronically mentally ill. They must learn to accept not only a diagnostic label but also the prospect of permanent impairment. This learning does not come easily.

3

Facing Chronicity

If only he had a job and friends again . . . so that he could be a happy person again. Do you see many cases where this could happen, or is this a pipe dream? . . . Can a person who's been this sick make a life for himself?

These are some of the questions that families ask themselves and professionals. The family is uncertain about its relative's capacity for any kind of happiness, yet it clings to the possibility that someday things will somehow get better. In some cases this is not to be. This chapter deals with common reactions to the evidence that the condition is chronic and describes what can realistically be expected of the chronically mentally ill.

The Mourning Process
The first stage in formulating appropriate expectations is to face the idea that the illness is permanent. Some families come to accept the idea of chronicity only after repeated crises or a very lengthy hospitalization. One father talked about this ac-

ceptance after his daughter had spent considerable time in a state hospital.

> I would never have thought when we came in that she would be here today, but as time has gone along . . . She had that spurt in the first year when she reached a fairly high level and that was encouraging, but then, of course, we saw her go downhill again.

A family can have many different emotions as it learns and begins to accept that its relative's illness will be long-term. Persistent sorrow is a frequent and often overwhelming feeling. The result of a significant change in the affected family member and the shattered hopes and expectations that follow this chronic illness have been described by family members as an experience analogous to mourning someone's death.

> It was really like a period of mourning, and I realized that it was. It was giving up the goals and the picture of her as a normal adult functioning, working at a library, which had been her dream. I think that's what it was—giving up that picture of her as an adult.

This sorrow reflects the pain of losing someone as you knew him and learning to adjust to stresses, limitations, and lost dreams. Most chronically ill persons are also chronically disabled. They never quite fulfill the promise they had shown. It is as if the healthy, "normal" individual with all the associated hopes and expectations had died. In that person's place is a stranger whose future is less certain, less hopeful, and whose present is tumultuous and painful. Even those people who recover satisfactorily have in some ways changed.

While the mourning process reflects a loss, it can also relieve you of the past and enable you to work toward the future. As you may recall in Chapter 1, Tom and Betty had difficulty in accepting the idea that Steve would never become "a new man." Eventually they learned to alter their expectations of him and to set new goals. Recognition and acceptance of the ill member as he is *now* allows you to live together with less pressure and tension.

The following account is the result of a discussion among three mental health professionals, two of whom have schizophrenic siblings. Both of the affected siblings have been ill for a number of years, though they are only in their twenties.

As the reality of the situation begins to sink in, you begin to realize that the person you had seen growing up, in whom you had hope, for whom you had expectations for a good life, is not going to make it; the potential that you had seen is not going to be tapped. Talents, such as woodworking or athletics, are overwhelmed by the mental disorder. Instead of growing up, maturing, and realizing everyone's expectations, the ill relative seems to fall apart as others his age pass him by.

The emotions you feel in this sort of situation are very similar to those experienced at the death of someone close to you. Some family members may feel that chronic mental illness is actually worse than death. Though it may sound harsh and cruel, that is a common feeling. This does not mean you wish your relative were dead. Rather, it expresses the pain you feel in seeing someone close to you living physically, but psychologically dead in many ways.

Living continually with a chronically ill individual ensures that you maintain a little bit of hope, no matter how ill the person. It is difficult to obtain a final peacefulness. There are many times, for example, that you might wish that a deceased relative were alive again. Unlike just wishing or thinking this about a dead person, you actually see your mentally ill relative; the person is really there. You sit in the car together, you go places and do things together, but all the while it is not the relative you once knew. The conflict between physical life and dead hopes is constantly there.

The mourning process allows you to face your anger and fear and to recognize your sadness. It can provide you with the strength to deal with the affected family member far more effectively. No small part of successful mourning is the personal relief it can give family members. Though you always suffer somewhat with chronic mental disability in the family, recognizing and coping with your depression can reduce some of the day-to-day hurt.

There are different ways to start facing the depression. Close friends who are willing to talk about the ill relative can be very helpful, particularly those who knew the family member before he or she became ill. They can share your loss, since they understand the changes. Family groups and competent therapists can also help. The important thing is to face the simple truth that chronic mental disability is sad; the sense of loss will come out in one way or another.

Unfortunately, long-term sorrow among families with a chronically disabled member is often interpreted by professionals as unhealthy or pathological. "The reason you experience a loss is that you expect too much," they may say, or "If you were more realistic, you wouldn't feel so sad." However the phrases are formed, the professional message is clear—you really have no reason to feel depressed. By either their silence or their accusations, professionals may fail to legitimize the family's feelings, further exacerbating an already difficult problem.

We do not intend to suggest that chronic sorrow is good or that you should feel depressed regularly. Rather, it is a fact that some families do feel this way. Although the realities of life are good reasons for sadness, persistent and intense sorrow is ultimately disruptive and interferes with successful adjustment. However, your sorrow and sense of loss cannot be brought under control if they are hidden away. It is natural both to feel and to express your depression. Indeed, it is important that you do so in order to go on living effectively.

One strategy to reduce the sense of loss is to think about today. Depression often results when you take a long-term view of life. Diana often thinks about what a good athlete and carpenter her brother had been and what he could have done in life had he not developed schizophrenia. Comparison with others' development and accomplishments often accompany these periods. Not surprisingly, the "big picture" in this case emphasizes the loss and makes the sadness more acute. However, when she plans an activity with her brother, fixes up the apartment, and helps him get a part-time job, she is less likely to feel the loss and more likely to derive pleasure from smaller, immediate gain.

Developing a Prognosis

In addition to emotional reactions to chronicity, you will probably have numerous questions. A consistent concern expressed to professionals is, "What is the prognosis? Will my relative ever get better?" This is an extremely difficult question for practitioners to answer, and many avoid doing so. Any answer given, of course, must be highly individualized, depending on that person's particular symptoms and his or her response to treatment. The following are some factors that are generally taken into consideration by professionals who attempt to specify a prognosis.

The individual's premorbid history can help determine future adjustment. "Premorbid" refers to the time period prior to the illness's first manifestations. If an individual becomes ill in his or her early teens, interrupting the normal process of development, the adjustment following the acute phase of the illness is usually more difficult than if the illness occurred later in life. In addition, if the individual has a long history of problems with school and friends and of conflicts at home, the future picture is less optimistic. Someone who has always experienced problems in relationships with others will only encounter more difficulty when the effects of a chronic mental illness are added. On the other hand, someone who experiences his first episode of depression during adulthood and who prior to that time had successfully held a job might find subsequent adjustment easier. The fact that this individual had not had an interruption of the normal growth toward independence that occurs during the teen years makes a better prognosis somewhat more likely.

Another factor that is essential in predicting prognosis is the individual's response to treatment and willingness to maintain the treatment regimen. Some people seem to have a poor response to treatment and spend longer periods of time in the hospital, while others improve quickly and return to normal functioning with fairly little disruption of their lives. Also, many individuals discontinue treatment for various reasons. These individuals will be less likely to make a satisfactory adjustment.

A significant issue in prognosis is what supports are available to the individual from family and peers, and what resources exist in the community. A primary problem for the chronically mentally ill has been the lack of appropriate housing and support services in the community. Many individuals could live on a semi-independent basis if there was adequate supervised housing. There are some programs available that offer this kind of twenty-four-hour support, but they are far too few to accommodate all those who would benefit from them. Even follow-up for medication and therapy is not always as accessible as it should be. Thus, as we have seen, the families shoulder the responsibility for the welfare of their relatives. The emotional support that you give, whether it is occasional contact or more continual involvement, may improve your relative's chance for survival and, beyond that, for a more comfortable life. One mother looked back on years of devotion to her ill daughter, who still remained hospitalized, and realized that even though her effort may not have substantially improved her condition, it had given her daughter some solace. As she said, "It's just as though anybody else in the family had an illness of any kind and they needed some human contact."

Even taking all the aforementioned factors into account,

mental health practitioners can only guess about your relative's future. They can only tell you what generally occurs. Your relative may not fit into this particular pattern.

Searching for a Miracle Cure

Regardless of what they are told, many families cannot accept the idea that their relative may never get significantly better.

> Each time there was that great white hope—maybe this time she'll stay on a fairly even keel, you can live with it. And when it didn't . . . I realized it's just a chronic thing. There isn't going to be any miracle cure.

Chronic mental illness is a frustrating and disappointing process to watch. An individual can experience a good remission of symptoms and then, due to stress, failure to take medication, or some spontaneous process, have a relapse. Sometimes the deterioration is observable over a considerable length of time, but occasionally it is abrupt. All too frequently an individual can experience a "roller-coaster" course of illness of several acute episodes interspersed with periods of symptom remission. The "up" periods can be deceiving and overly heartening to those families who view their relative as "cured" and who expect or hope that the illness will never reappear.

One mother expected such a cure to occur because she was working so hard to make it happen. In all other circumstances of her life, she had been able to control situations because she made the effort to do so.

> I kept thinking . . . if we all worked together it would be okay. Here I am in *Alice in Wonderland* . . . I felt in my heart that if we all worked at it, we would work her out of it . . . Most of all, because I'm a very determined person . . . I feel there's nothing in the world that if I work hard enough I won't get.

Many families express this hope: If only enough people put enough thought and energy into helping the relative, the illness would be eradicated and life would return to normal. When they (or the relative) are not able to attain a cure through sheer will power and effort, they are enormously frustrated, disappointed, and angry. Sometimes this anger is experienced as guilt that they have somehow not done enough. At other times they blame the relative, whom they see as simply not working hard enough to make himself or herself well.

Some families expect this same magical power from mental health practitioners. Professionals are seen as healers who can certainly, through their expertise, effect a cure. Families are often so desperate to put their trust into someone and to get some optimistic outlook that they view professionals as more powerful than they actually are. In our society we are taught to see doctors or healers as all-powerful and all-knowing. We expect them to be able to help no matter what the problem. We react with disbelief and anger when we find that they do not have all the answers and cannot make everything better. This attitude carries over into the mental health field, and many families are convinced that if they find the suitable treatment facility or the "best" mental health practitioner, they will have found a lasting solution to their relatives' problems.

This expectation of cure frequently leads to an endless search for better hospitals, different treatments, and more competent professionals. It can make the family vulnerable to unproven and "fad" treatments. Megavitamin therapy is an example of one such therapy which many families turn to in desperation but which has not yet been satisfactorily researched and substantiated. It is certainly undeniable that there are, in fact, different levels of competence among professionals and mental health facilities, and differentially effective treatments. Families often use this disparity, however, to convince themselves that someone somewhere will have *the* answer. There is no question that you should seek out competence, understanding, and forthrightness. What you must avoid is the tendency to seek constantly something better instead of reaching some acceptance that it is the nature of the illness and our current knowledge that prohibit a cure.

If you do wish to explore different treatment opportunities, the time to do so is not when your relative is doing well and making satisfactory strides. Since a remission can be precarious, introducing unnecessary change is unwise. If, on the other hand, no progress is being made after quite a lengthy try with one method or professional, or deterioration has actually begun, you might take that opportunity to try a different approach. In your search remember again that while medication, therapy, and environment can all have a significant impact on chronic mental illness, there is no cure. There can be relief from symptoms such as a diabetic achieves through insulin. But the diabetes and the mental illness are still present, and the symptoms can return.

Relapses

A family who has accepted the chronicity of its relative's condition may still find the specter of continued acute episodes quite frightening. "I'm so concerned this time," one parent said, "because I can't see anything happening except that she's going to keep meeting defeat after defeat after defeat." The family may continue to become discouraged after each setback, always wondering if the situation will get worse. When the relative is ill, the family may wonder if the relative will ever again experience a "good" period. When he or she is functioning reasonably well, it awaits with dread the possibility of deterioration. There can be an almost daily fear of what the next day, week, or month will bring. Tom Lacey comments on his wife's constant apprehension: "[She] got up in the morning yesterday, and she says, 'What's gonna happen today?' Six-thirty in the morning and she's gotta tell me, 'What's gonna happen today?'"

Some of this dread can be alleviated by having some idea of

what to expect, even if it is not what you hoped for. It is likely that an individual with chronic mental illness will have relapses. One acute episode or one hospitalization is the exception rather than the norm. When your relative leaves the hospital and functions well in the community for a time, you should not build up hopes that there will never be another admission. If you can mentally prepare yourself for ups and downs, you can guard, at least in part, against undue disappointment and frustration. You can hope for shorter hospitalizations with longer intervals of adequate functioning in the community. Some individuals are able, through a series of hospitalizations, to gradually increase their stay in the community, so that the time out becomes longer than the time in. If the time spent in the community is rewarding, then some gains have been achieved no matter what develops in the future. One young woman who had many hospitalizations was finally able to stay in the community for several years. She held a job, made friends, and began to regain her self-confidence. This period became the most satisfying time for her since her illness had first begun, five years before. In pondering the possibility of a relapse sometime in the future, she felt that she could tolerate a setback and that it would not be as devastating as previous relapses had been. She attributed this to her newfound self-esteem and to her discovery that she could make a satisfying life for herself. She was convinced that this knowledge could sustain her through another acute episode and that the progress she had made would not be lost.

Institutionalization

An oft-voiced concern of the family whose relative is hospitalized for a long period of time (a few months or more) is whether the relative will become "institutionalized." One mother spoke of her fear about her son's lengthy hospital stay even though she knew he needed long-term treatment: "I struggle with the idea of institutionalization making a person more chronic."

Institutionalization can result in a lack of motivation and caring about personal hygiene, daily activities, or the long-range future. Individuals who spend considerable time in the hospital frequently do not feel that there is any reason for them to care about how they look or act. They may demonstrate very poor table manners, eating quite sloppily and hurriedly with no attention to social conversation during the meal. Similarly, they may lose interest in events in the outside world. They become comfortable and secure in the structure and routine of the hospital setting. Demands are minimal and they can avoid taking risks. Since they have lost practice in coping with any kinds of demands, they feel unable to keep up with the responsibilities of noninstitutional living.

If your relative's acute illness is treatable in a short period of time and if your relative has a place to return to in the community, then a shorter hospital stay is preferable. This is not always possible. The individual's illness may not respond quickly to treatment. The current cost of private hospitals may drain a family's funds, and the individual may be moved to a state hospital. Such a move may slow down the return to the community: A new period of observation is required in this new setting, and your relative may go through another period of adjustment to the new treatment personnel. The individual may not have a suitable environment to which he can return and may need assistance in locating a job or housing, which may delay his release. Some people do need and benefit from longer hospitalizations: The pause from overwhelming responsibilities and the extended support from caring professionals can give them the emotional strength to return to the demands of daily life outside the hospital.

If, for whatever reason, your relative does require a longer inpatient period, you need not despair over his remaining in the hospital forever. While institutionalization may indeed occur to some degree, it is not irreversible. A family that is supportive and able to bolster its relative's self-confidence will be of tremendous help in offsetting this process. It is also extremely important for you to help your relative maintain contact with the community by encouraging activity outside the security of the hospital. If the hospital is not the only world in which your relative functions, there is less chance that a paralyzing dependency on that setting will develop. Those situations that we handle frequently are less likely to make us fearful and uncertain.

One young woman who had been hospitalized for ten years with one brief, unsuccessful attempt in the community had given up any interest in leaving the hospital. There she had activities to keep her busy, friends, and easy access to supportive professionals. Every time anyone mentioned to her the possibility of leaving, she became tense and agitated and experienced an increase in the depressive symptoms that had originally led to her hospitalization. Both the woman and her family were concerned about her apparent lack of motivation to leave the hospital, but no one wanted to push her toward a recurrence of her acute depression. Everyone began to wonder if she would ever leave the hospital.

Eventually, with the support of her family and the hospital staff, this woman was able to make a satisfactory adjustment into the community. The major factor in her successfully leaving the hospital was the gradual resumption of outside activities. At first she was accompanied on shopping excursions into the community so that she could learn the transportation system and feel less self-conscious outside the protective environs of the hospital. As she gained self-confidence, she began to attend a two-day-a-week program at a day hospital in the community. Following that, she obtained a job but continued to return to the hospital for evenings and weekends. Finally she rented an apartment near her family and moved out of the hospital. She continued to see friends from the hospital and continued her therapy with a hospital psychologist until she made the transition to a therapist at her local mental health center. The gradual and supportive process enabled this woman to slowly gather her energies and her coping resources to overcome her fright. Her family's encouragement and assistance were invaluable in providing opportunities to be in the community and in making these occasions rewarding.

Burnout

Some chronically ill individuals eventually "slow down." They experience fewer acute episodes, and their particularly active and destructive behavior lessens. They become less assaultive and less self-destructive and have fewer violent outbursts. This desirable decrease in disruptive behavior is often accompanied by an undesirable increase in apathy, isolation, and complacency. The illness is said to have "burned out." This phenomenon usually occurs after numerous acute episodes and as the person gets older, perhaps in the late thirties or forties. It can also accompany particularly lengthy hospitalizations. Burnout certainly does not occur with everyone and is not a necessary outcome of chronic mental illness.

Although you might look forward to a time when your relative is less agitated, you might be understandably frightened that your relative will become withdrawn. You may be particularly concerned because you have seen chronic patients in the hospital who seem to spend day after day rocking and staring vacantly at the television set. However, it should be comforting to realize that for an individual who has been suffering for a long time with internal turmoil, this "slowing down" can provide much-needed calm, and it need not be accompanied by a total lack of activity. Supportive family members and caring professionals may be able to reduce the degree of apathy by providing opportunities for accomplishment and enjoyment.

Planning for the Future

Chronic mental illness has a definite impact on your ability to plan for both the immediate and the more distant future.

The inability to make short-range plans results in more and more isolation as families hesitate to make arrangements that could be disrupted. As we have seen, social life becomes restricted and recreational activities infrequent. Family life is characterized by living from one crisis to another. The lack of long-range visions makes existence seem empty, devoid of the usual goals and dreams that make our lives interesting.

You need not give up totally your wish to plan or to instill some order into your life. One way to accomplish these is to plan smaller units of time. If tomorrow is too uncertain, perhaps the next two hours are not. You may also find that you are less disappointed by the interruption of activities that have taken less effort and preparation.

Expectations and goals also can be readjusted. Perhaps the dreams are less auspicious than those originally formulated, but they can still fulfill the longing to make plans for the future. Betty Lacey summarizes her adjustment:

> I don't hope for the things I hoped for before. I just hope that Steve can take care of his own personal needs, that alone. I wish my husband and I could help him more, but we won't be able to do that, I know that, too . . . At least now I don't expect too much . . . This way I'm not as disappointed, and if he does make any progress, at least . . . that's extra.

Betty has accepted the reduction of goals and at the same time has protected herself from constant disappointment. In this way Steve's achievements, however small, can be greeted as "bonuses," as real accomplishments that are accepted with pleasure but are not demanded of him.

A family can doom itself to disappointment if it holds on to the hope of a profession for someone with a serious thinking disorder or of a marriage and family for someone who fears intimacy and lacks good social skills. Satisfaction can be derived when expectations are more in line with the ill member's abilities.

43

Avoiding Hopelessness

One mother talks about the feelings of hopelessness that come so easily with the endless disappointments:

> I know you can't give up hope. We still read with interest [about] drugs that are being used and that kind of thing. But the feeling of hopelessness is so overwhelming and it's so hard to get out of. You just realize you can't let yourself get into that kind of thing. It'll destroy you.

Hopelessness can be pervasive. It may be communicated by professionals whose knowledge of the variability of the illness makes them cautious in expressing any optimism. After all, professionals generally see the individuals who are having difficulties coping, and they have little opportunity to see the individuals who have made successful adjustments. Professionals may warn the family that it should not expect anything from the relative, that it should give up any notions that the relative can lead even a marginally normal life.

The ill individual himself may give up after repeated failures and may not wish to strive after any further goals. His withdrawal and lack of motivation may gradually convince the family that all it or anyone else can provide is custodial care.

You, too, can easily feel hopeless after you witness several hospitalizations and what appears to be the endless misery of your relative. You despair that all the time and energy you have put in have not turned your relative's life around. Families like the Laceys who have constantly altered their expectations to avoid disappointment may be particularly susceptible to this sense of hopelessness. The chronicity can rob both the ill individual and the family of any hopes that the future will be better.

In spite of all the pressure to the contrary, many families do not give up. In the face of what often seem like insurmountable odds, they continue to hope. They do not deny the chronic nature of the illness, but they refuse to give up the idea that at some point their ill relatives will lead constructive lives. These families admit a gap between their intellectual knowledge of the illness and their emotional longings. One mother described her feelings of disappointment when she finally realized just how chronic her daughter's illness was, but added:

> I don't know even to this minute if I accept it. It's very easy to sit and say, "I accept that." But those are words. I don't really know yet if deep down inside I accept that.

You need to hope in order to continue to help. Chronic illness is not improved by chronic pessimism. Hope enables you to maintain involvement with your relative, to persevere in seeking adequate treatment, and to provide opportunities for your relative to meet with success. No one can take away that hope. Realistically, there are indeed many chronically ill individuals who do make the necessary adjustments that enable them to lead full lives. Further research may discover more successful treatments. And finally, improvement in services provided by the mental health system can have a significant impact. Hope sustains not only the family but also the ill individual. Your relative's realistic hopes can provide the incentive to face the hard work and sacrifice that can lead to a more fulfilling life.

II

UNDERSTANDING
YOUR FEELINGS

4

Guilt

All of us have regrets. We wish we had a chance to relive parts of our lives—to make different choices, to experience different results. Many of these wishes concern how we have behaved with various people over the years. When someone we care most about—a parent, a spouse, or a child—has a chronic mental illness, our sense of responsibility enlarges those regrets until it seems as if a cloud covers each potential joy. Recurrent thoughts about the past often hinder families of the mentally ill in functioning effectively in the present.

An Illustration

Sue and Dan had three children. The oldest, Karen, had been a pretty, bright, and good-tempered child. Although she had been somewhat shy and occasionally given to bouts of fearsome stomachaches, nothing in Karen's history prepared her parents for the seemingly senseless temper tantrums she began to have at age sixteen. Once she hurled an ashtray at her mother, who had done nothing more than ask her to dry the dinner dishes. On another occasion she slapped her sister, who had asked to borrow a record. Sue began to buy Karen's clothes for her, since Karen often appeared confused and agitated in stores and more than once had run tearfully to the car. She seemed unable to make even the simplest decisions.

Sue and Dan's attempts to discipline Karen—by withholding her allowance, grounding her, or slapping her—were met with childlike apologies. Nevertheless, Karen's behavior grew steadily worse. She continued to fly into rages for no apparent reason, and her parents and siblings found themselves becoming more and more careful of what they said to her. Within a year she was capable of terrorizing the household for days on end.

When she was almost eighteen, Karen met a young man she wanted to marry. Her parents were concerned, as he had no job, had left his family, and appeared very jealous and possessive. Yet in the hopes that marriage might settle her down, they reluctantly consented. In truth, as they later admitted, they were glad to be relieved of the burden of her care.

Their burden, however, only increased. Karen returned home almost daily to complain that her husband refused to give her money to buy food, locked her out of the house, and hit her repeatedly. Dan had several heart-to-heart talks with the young man, who denied Karen's accusations and professed to be perplexed and overwhelmed by Karen's odd behavior. On her nineteenth birthday, Karen shot herself in the stomach to get rid of an unborn child that existed only in her imagination. Karen eventually made an excellent physical recovery, but she continues to need psychiatric care.

Sue and Dan, like so many other parents, blamed themselves and each other. Both searched endlessly for some error in their behavior that would account for Karen's illness. Was it that Dan, wanting a son, had taught Karen rough tomboy sports? Was it that Sue had neglected Karen in favor of her charitable activities? Was it that they had slapped her too often? Not often enough? Their conversations ranged over every incident they could remember, scrutinizing each for some evidence of error.

Both parents agreed that they should have realized the severity of Karen's problems much earlier. Instead, they had called her willful and rebellious. They had believed her attacks of temper reflected nothing more than a normal, if difficult, adolescence. Both also felt tremendously guilty that they had consented to her marriage, blaming themselves for responding to their own relief rather than to thoughts of Karen's welfare.

Despair, guilt, and anger at each other drove Sue and Dan further and further apart. They were unable to talk to each other without strain. Afraid that they might make the same unknown mistakes again, they unconsciously withdrew from their two healthy children. Dan no longer engaged in playful wrestling. Sue no longer required that the children help with household chores.

At the same time, Karen's brother and sister needed more support than ever. Each secretly felt responsible for what had happened to Karen, and each interpreted their parents' inattentive behavior as confirmation of guilt. They felt that they had been selfish, jealous children and that their parents no longer loved them. Dinner time became a silent, painful experience for everyone.

Wanting desperately to make up to Karen for their imagined errors, her parents were unable to provide the limits and control necessary to her rehabilitation. They could not bring themselves to insist that she participate in needed therapeutic activities. When she came home from the hospital for visits, they catered to her needs and fulfilled every request. They made no demands. Paradoxically, Dan and Sue, who tried so hard to give their daughter everything she needed, only succeeded in removing the opportunity for her to develop increased independence and competence.

This family's story is far from unusual. Since the specific causes of most mental illnesses are largely unknown, it is natural to search for an explanation that lies within the family environment. Family members blame themselves, each other, their ill relative, and others in their attempts to make some sense out of what has happened. Indeed, in such families guilt is often a measure of the love and concern felt for the disturbed member. While guilt is rarely useful, the love it reflects can be a powerful source of support for the individual and for the family as a whole. In exploring the most common sources of familial guilt, we hope to show that family members' behavior is rarely, if ever, the cause of chronic mental illness, and that most past incidents can be thought about in a new light.

Sources of Guilt

Dan and Sue suspected that they must have been bad parents. They, like other parents, had read that their behavior was crucial to the emotional well-being of their children. The press had popularized Freud's notion of trauma, according to which any parental misstep, however minor, could severely damage a child emotionally. It was impossible to know how to rear children. Too much attention, too little attention, too much discipline, too little discipline—any behavior could have long-lasting effects. Having done the best they could, they presumed that their best had not been good enough. Their own experience revealed that many children successfully weathered severe family conflict and that many others developed serious problems even in the most nurturing atmosphere. In their own case, the weight of professional opinion appeared to be against them, namely that they "drove Karen crazy."

However, much scientific evidence suggests that the family's role in the development of serious mental illness in one of its members has been exaggerated. First, it is now believed that many mental illnesses, including schizophrenia, childhood autism, alcoholism, and certain of the depressions, have a genetic component. In other words, some people are physically predisposed to develop these illnesses, and other people are not. The role of the environment, including that of the family, in the appearance of symptoms is nonspecific; that is, any environmental event that is stressful will increase the immediate chances that a susceptible person will develop psychiatric symptoms. Thus, while inappropriate discipline, parental conflicts, and inadequate family communication can act as stressors, they constitute a very small number of potentially stressful situations to which all of us may be exposed. Further, *all* families are sources of stress for their members. Since individuals differ from each other in their needs, goals, values, interests, and personality styles, a certain amount of conflict naturally exists within each family unit.

It is entirely possible that a major psychiatric illness will develop in the individual whose family has provided a supportive, low-stress environment if he is biologically at risk and subjected to other environmental pressures. Some people may have such a strong predisposition that the disorder will develop in *any* environment. Further, even when the family structure is stressful to its members, it is unlikely that this alone will precipitate a chronic psychiatric problem in individuals with no biological predisposition. While family members can cause each other emotional pain and can interfere with the maximal development of various life skills, chronic mental illness often reflects a biochemical illness over which the family has limited, if any, control.

Second, although Freud's idea of the damaging trauma has been used extensively to explain events *after* they occur, there is no evidence that we can predict that a certain event will have a specific outcome. A punishment, for example, may have a beneficial effect in one instance and not in another, depending upon how the punishment is given, the previous history of punishments, the emotional and social climate in which the punishment takes place, and the personality traits of the person being punished. The effect of withholding a child's allowance, for example, depends upon how important the money is to the child, how well "the punishment fits the crime," how often allowance has been withheld in the past, and whether the child perceives the punishment as constructive or spiteful. It is senseless to label a particular bit of parental, spouse, or child behavior as "bad" out of context. Thus, for the large majority of family behaviors, the worst that can be said is that a particular behavior is not useful and does not achieve the desired result in a specific situation.

Finally, many of us think of children as fragile, malleable creatures who are totally at the mercy of the environment. This is certainly not true; they differ from birth in activity level, fearfulness, and general mood. Children affect their environment as well as being affected by it, so that particular patterns of family interaction develop in accordance with both parents' and children's traits.

Now let us look again at Dan and Sue's behavior. Did Dan make Karen sick by treating her more like a son than a daughter? Some children would thrive on this kind of close contact and attention from their fathers, while other, less active children might feel overwhelmed by the demands of rough-and-tumble sports. Karen might have become confused about her identity as a girl, but only if Sue had also provided a poor role model. Regardless, it is highly unlikely that Dan's behavior could account for the later development of Karen's chronic mental illness. It is impossible even to evaluate Dan's behavior without considering Karen's individual ways of responding, as well as the larger family and social contexts.

Did Sue make Karen sick by being away from home frequently? An independent child might profit from some time away from mother's watchful eye, while a fearful child might feel insecure. If the time spent apart made Sue and Karen enjoy their time together more, the separations might have been beneficial. If Sue had been generally withdrawn, the separations might have made Karen feel even worse. In general, the quality of parent/child interactions is at least as important as the quantity of those interactions. Did Sue leave Karen with someone who was affectionate and playful, or with someone who only watched her? This would make a difference as well.

Again, the effects of Sue's absences cannot be evaluated without reference to the context in which they occurred. Many busy working mothers raise healthy and happy children. Some do not. Many devoted, stay-at-home mothers raise healthy and happy children. Some do not.

It is unlikely that any particular relative's behavior could account, by itself, for a subsequent serious mental illness. Karen's biological, familial, and social environment were all involved in complex ways. Families ought to give up their search for the crucial mistake. It does not exist.

Sue and Dan were particularly distressed about their failure to realize that Karen was sick before she shot herself. They thought, in retrospect, that her temper tantrums were a sign that she needed help and that even her childhood stomachaches were evidence of illness that they had overlooked. Many times parents and spouses of mentally ill persons feel most guilty over misinterpreting the signs of impending problems. However, as we mentioned in Chapter 2, missing such signs is a normal thing to do.

Many of the early signs of mental illness are quite subtle. They may include social withdrawal, moodiness, excessive drinking or drug use, crying spells, and other stress-related behaviors. It is often only through hindsight that they can be seen as "signs" of oncoming illness.

Thus, Karen's stomachaches were naturally, and probably correctly, seen by her parents as relatively unimportant responses to stress. Her adolescent tantrums were interpreted as evidence of attempts to achieve independence so typical of that stage of development. The fantasy-based accusations against her husband that indicated that Karen was losing contact with reality went unexamined by her parents because they chose, again quite normally, to believe her explanations rather than her husband's. Confused by conflicting accounts, they attempted to let the young couple find their own solutions. Karen's family behaved like the majority of other families might under the same circumstances. They chose the most likely explanations for the various changes they observed. They simply did not have all the information they needed to act more effectively.

Another common source of guilt is the anger family members felt in response to behavior that was later seen to be out of the disturbed relative's control. Thus, Karen's parents felt guilty about having punished her for temper tantrums, having felt relieved when she got married, and having felt burdened by her constant complaints about her husband. They had conceived of her as willful, stubborn, and selfish rather than as ill. They had mislabeled her behavior as "bad" rather than "mad," and had treated her accordingly. Guilty about their unspoken thoughts as well as their behavior, they were later unable to set realistic expectations for Karen or for their other two children. Having expected too much, they later expected too little.

It is normal for parents to have angry thoughts about their children and for siblings and spouses to be angry with each other. Such feelings do not make you an ogre, only a human being. When balanced by concern and love, they are part of a full emotional relationship. If family members could remember their times of caring, nurturance, and selflessness as well as their angry and hostile ones, they would have a more accurate and less painful understanding of the past.

Natural feelings of remorse and guilt are heightened and perpetuated by the response of the community. Just as mental patients are shunned by many people, so the families of the chronically mentally ill are sometimes ostracized by extended family and friends. Others may experience irrational fears of contagion, uncertainty about how to respond to the family's problems, worries about running into the ill family member, and suspicions that other family members may be disturbed or at fault. Thus, the invitations, visits, and phone calls that would follow physical illness in the family are absent or limited in the families of the mentally ill. Family members stigmatized and isolated in this way cannot help but feel blamed and punished.

Effects of Guilt

Guilt leads to depression and robs people of self-confidence and strength, often paralyzing individuals and even whole families. People who believe themselves to be incompetent or blameworthy are less able to initiate new activities, solve problems, and achieve goals. A vicious cycle can easily develop in which deepening guilt decreases the ability to cope effectively, which leads in turn to ever more pervasive feelings of personal worthlessness. Guilty people are also more likely to martyr themselves needlessly. In a futile attempt to erase the mistakes of the past, they make constant sacrifices in the present. Martyr behavior is rarely helpful and can be harmful when the recipient is made to feel helplessly dependent or as if he owes a huge debt of gratitude he can never repay. Guilt can also lead to overprotectiveness. Recall that Sue and Dan felt so guilty about having misinterpreted Karen's behavior that later they were unable to set the limits necessary for her rehabilitation.

Self-defeating guilt is particularly dangerous in families with a mentally ill member. Such families cannot afford to remain mired in the past; they will need all of their emotional resources to live from day to day and to plan for the future. Guilt of the kinds we have described pulls families apart when they most need to be together and saps energy when energy is most needed.

Although we have pointed out how fruitless and irrational most of these guilty feelings are, we know that families with a mentally ill member are bound to experience them. It is virtually impossible not to. While guilt may never completely vanish, it need not remain a constant companion. The question of what one did wrong cannot be answered with certainty, but family members are usually harder on themselves than the available scientific evidence indicates they ought to be. Most family members have done the best they could with the emotional and informational resources they had available; they are not to be blamed for the illness in their midst.

UNDERSTANDING YOUR FEELINGS

When you find yourself feeling guilty or engaging in behavior whose sole purpose is to reduce your guilt, you can first examine the beliefs that are causing your guilt. Are you telling yourself that you *should* have known? Are you angry at yourself for having behaved just like anyone else might have under the circumstances? When you are able to pinpoint the irrational, guilt-provoking belief, try arguing with yourself forcefully and assertively using the relevant information from this chapter. If you practice, you will find yourself developing more rational, less painful ways of thinking about your situation. Rather than dwell on the past, families can work toward a focus on present concerns and future possibilities.

5

Anger

Anger is an emotion with which we are all familiar. Many of us recall times when we have "seethed with fury," been "blind with anger" or "purple with rage." The heart beats rapidly, a flush may appear on the face, and breathing may become rapid and shallow. Under such conditions, we not only feel anger but also wish to attack the object of our anger. Some people rarely, if ever, have these intense physical experiences but, rather, feel a quiet anger. Instead of shouting and throwing things, they become sullen and sarcastic. Others avoid their angry feelings for fear of losing control. Rather than risk confrontation, they withdraw. This strategy controls anger but also dampens other emotions so that those people feel life less intensely.

Sometimes anger is an outgrowth of the guilt felt by families of the chronically mentally disabled. Filled with constant remorse and useless hindsights, they feel helpless to resolve these feelings. This unresolved guilt turns into anger, which can at least find expression and provide some release. But the expression of the anger often backfires, resulting in increased guilt, more anger, and so on.

These families have many targets for their anger: the ill person, themselves, mental health and legal professionals, and society at large. Often the anger is appropriate; just as often it hinders the family's effectiveness. In some instances family members feel a general hostility that seeks expression but cannot find appropriate channels. No matter how it is expressed or at whom directed, anger is an emotion with which we must come to grips. For families of the chronically mentally ill, this may be a difficult task, but one that must be accomplished for the benefit of everyone concerned.

The Many Targets of Anger

Very few family members living with chronic mental disability escape anger. Early in the family's difficulties the ill person himself may elicit the irritability and hostility of the other family members. Once the seriousness of the disability is confirmed, family members often turn upon each other in an attempt to place the blame for mental illness. As the long-term responsibility and uncertainty about the ill person's future begin to emerge, anger may be directed vaguely at the whole situation. No one person is the "bad guy" so much as fate for having condemned the family to a lifelong burden. Finally, and often appropriately, families turn against professionals for their failure to provide the information and support essential to the task.

One of the most difficult forms of anger with which families must cope is that felt toward the ill person himself. There are many aspects of mental illness that can make people angry. Betty found it very hard to ignore her son's irrational beliefs "when he was into voodoo or whatever. That used to make me mad because I couldn't stand that, when he believed in witchcraft and all that."

Sometimes the anger runs deep and a family member is hurt for a long time. The daughter of an alcoholic mother described the following:

She didn't see my wedding gown until the day before the wedding. She wanted nothing to do with it. She wouldn't go and get it with me. I don't think I've ever forgiven her for that one. I mean, somewhere deep inside I don't think I've ever forgiven her. She refused to sign for the wedding . . . She wasn't even going to the wedding . . . I was angry and very hurt.

The Laceys had to face angry outbursts from their son, to watch as their other child was teased and irritated, and to struggle to maintain control of their own household. To have a family member consistently and aggressively ignore the rights of the rest of the family in such a manner as loudly playing the stereo at three in the morning is enough to make anyone angry. The families of the chronically mentally ill are only responding naturally under the circumstances. Furthermore, the fact is that even the saintliest behavior fails to stop chronic mental disability.

Many families report that a diagnosis and information about the mental disability help them to view the ill family member in a new way and to ease tension. Anger lessens when family members know that the ill person often does things that are not under his control and that are not done intentionally to hurt anyone. As the daughter of the alcoholic mother points out:

My thoughts were then [upon learning that her mother suffered from alcoholism] that the drinking upset some sort of mental balance, and it was a mental problem. The alcoholic problem gave me whatever I needed to say, "It's okay, I forgive you."

While understanding goes a long way in dissipating anger, it is also true that years of emotions cannot simply be erased. A younger brother of a schizophrenic felt he could not eliminate feelings sustained for years by waving the "magic wand of diagnosis." It is quite natural to feel some remnants of the anger and hostility that may have existed before the family learned that mental illness was the cause of disruptive behavior. The knowledge provides a new perspective that allows families to respond to annoying, irritating behavior with some detachment.

Even if family members understand and accept the idea of mental disability, the road is still not clear; inevitably there will be instances in which the ill person will do something that angers them.

As we shall discuss later, there are ways of dealing with your emotions and with the ill person that help to minimize friction. Generally, anytime family members can avoid direct, immediate emotional responses, the better off all concerned will be. When, for example, Steve Lacey turns his stereo up to full volume at three in the morning, the natural inclination is to shout angrily at Steve to turn the volume down. This type of response, however, will simply increase the chances for escalation. After counting to themselves for a few seconds (until they are calm), Tom and Betty might suggest to Steve that he use headphones at whatever volume he chooses. This response both allows Steve his freedom and protects the rights of the rest of the family.

There will be instances in which all the "right" things are said with no result and you become angry. The pitfall for families at this point is to blame themselves or to feel guilty for being angry at a sick person. Feeling this way does not make you a bad individual, only a human with a wide range of emotions—anger, hurt, and joy.

Sometimes families will have had enough of the day-to-day care and the seeming futility of their efforts. When they think ahead to a future of unending responsibility, they are especially likely to feel bitter about the condition dictated to them by fate. "Why don't the Smiths have a schizophrenic son?" "Why did it have to be my wife who is always depressed?" "Why don't I have normal parents like the other kids?"

In point of fact, there is no justice to the situation. Until we discover causes and cures of serious mental disability, families will suffer the hardships it imposes. It is natural to be "mad at the world" for this situation, but such anger can become all-consuming. If families spend so much time cursing fate that practical realities of everyday life are ignored, anger clearly is detrimental. There are many things families can do to modify their fate, but angrily talking about it accomplishes very little. No words will easily soothe this type of anger. Therefore, it is important to strive toward acceptance of the current circumstances. Psychologically "rolling up your sleeves" can be the best therapy.

The frustration, impatience, and anger with the ill relative that families may feel are sometimes expressed directly. When Tom Lacey yelled at Steve on one occasion, "he picked up a pitchfork and he just flung it at me." As in most instances of this sort, direct expression of anger just causes trouble for everyone.

More commonly, the anger leaks out in other, less obvious ways. One family, for example, may compare its ill member with others who are doing much better and who fulfill the hopes that may once have been held for the mentally disabled person. This sort of hostile critique often reflects anger and frustration. It is easy, for another example, to finish a task for which the ill person is responsible and to then remind him that you have once again helped him out. Though anger may not be consciously felt in such circumstances, the message clearly is one of "Why can't you do it yourself? I'm tired of always taking care of you."

It is precisely because chronic mental disability is a long-term responsibility that families will regularly be subject to indirect expressions of anger. We know that any chronic illness, whether it be diabetes, epilepsy, or schizophrenia, provokes anger at the unrelenting needs of the ill person as well as a sense of being trapped and of the unfairness of it all. However, families of the medically ill generally receive support and sympathy in one way: Their anger and frustration are seen as reasonable for their circumstances. Let a family of a mentally disabled person openly express negative emotions and it is seen as evidence of "family pathology." Despite this professional and social bias to view the family as troublemaker, anger is quite normal. By eliminating the surprise and recognizing that anger is to be expected, families can help themselves gain control over anger's expression.

Many times, other family members become convenient targets for anger. Since the others are healthy and share the responsibility for the ill person, it is easier to blame and angrily criticize them than to express anger toward the ill relative. This is especially likely when the anger family members might normally direct toward the ill relative is stifled. Consider, for example, the comic strip situation in which a person is soundly reprimanded by his boss. The employee, fearing for his job, does not fight back. Instead, he goes home and finds fault with his wife, children, and dog. The anger the person feels has been displaced from the appropriate target (his boss) to an inappropriate one (wife, children, and dog). Similarly, rather than be openly angry with the ill person, some family members displace their emotions to the other members of the family.

People can express their anger in different ways. Betty was frustrated and angry with herself; Tom went to his basement alone. Each was bothered by the other spouse's behavior. Betty wondered why Tom was withdrawn and uninvolved. Tom, for his part, could not understand why Betty would get so upset. Unless individual differences in emotional expression are understood and discussed, it is very likely that the end result will be to push family members apart.

For parents, this anger may involve differences in child-rearing practices. One mother of a chronically mentally ill daughter said:

It used to make me very angry. Her father would not make her do anything. Her father would make the other kids be hand-maidens and manservants, but he was frightened . . . for her to do anything.

Similarly, parents may accuse brothers and sisters of not being responsible enough and of failing to consider the ill person's point of view. In turn the nuclear family may band together in angrily denouncing the extended family for being too involved or not involved enough, for saying too little or too much.

Sometimes these reactions are quite appropriate. Betty Lacey was understandably angry when her father-in-law told her that Steve would come to no good. Under such circumstances it would be unusual not to feel angry. At other times healthy family members are simply more acceptable targets for your feelings than the ill person. After a particularly trying day with her son, Betty Lacey might well be overly angry with Tom for arriving home a few minutes late. In this case Betty expresses her anger at Steve by criticizing Tom.

Also, as captured by the age-old saying that "you hurt the ones you love," anger often is more easily expressed at those with whom you feel safe. However, it is important to control such feelings or to express them appropriately. While direct angry outbursts are a part of the human condition, they generally hurt more than they help.

Perhaps some of the most intense and persistent anger that families experience is directed at people and institutions outside the family. As was true in the case of the Laceys, anger is often appropriate. Different professionals gave them different opinions about Steve's problems, ranging from brain damage to absence of any disorder. Other professionals accused them of selfishness. When the Laceys turned to Steve's teachers for help in maintaining medication, they were refused. The principal once came to Betty Lacey's place of work to publicly complain about Steve. Anyone receiving this sort of treatment would be angry and rightly so.

Unanswered phone calls, accusations, vague answers, contradictory information, inadequate resources (such as housing and supplemental income), and lack of sympathy are all reported by families of the chronically mentally ill. Many families feel that they must fight a system that has given them nothing but trouble.

The community or society at large also attracts its share of anger from families. This is most likely to arise when the ill relative attempts to return to the community to live independently. When, however, the ill person is unable to abide by common social rules (as Steve Lacey was), then the community rejects the person. Many families are angry that "they" do not have more patience; if only "they" understood more about mental illness. Why cannot society be more tolerant? What if "their" relatives were ill?

For some people, anger becomes a way of life. Rather than constructively using the anger, they often feel aroused and seem to continually search for people at whom to be angry. Their anger interferes with personal relationships, causes friction, and further isolates them. The increased isolation and friction just make them angrier, producing a vicious cycle. It is always possible to find acceptable reasons for this type of anger, but the ultimate victim is the angry person. Alone, fighting, and seemingly never winning, the chronically angry person ends up hurting both himself and the ill relative.

Handling Anger

One way to avoid intense, uncontrollable anger is to express mild anger appropriately when it occurs. This is why recognizing your typical angry response is important. Trying to push anger aside or out of your mind does not work over the long run. Emotions get stored up and eventually emerge "out of the blue."

Consider a typical day in Betty Lacey's life. There are numerous things that might provoke her anger. Steve shouts at her, rushes out of the house, or annoys the neighbors. Rather than letting her temper go, she decides not to say anything about her feelings, hoping thereby to make the day go more smoothly. That evening, after dinner, Tom starts to go downstairs to his shop, as he frequently does. Tonight, as he starts to leave, Betty begins shouting at Tom for his withdrawal, his failure to help with Steve, his lack of housework, and his failure to give her support. From Tom's point of view, Betty's angry outburst is uncalled for. We can see, however, how Betty's anger had been accumulating all day. Like a balloon under constant inflation, she must sooner or later burst. It is possible to prevent these intense episodes through expression of milder anger at appropriate times.

But what is mild anger? How do you express your anger without hurting others or yourself? It is unbridled hostility and the sense of attack that usually creates problems. Therefore, it is helpful to keep a handle on your anger. You can do this in two ways—by giving yourself time to cool down and by separating what has made you angry from the person who did it.

Let us suppose that Steve Lacey has thrown out all of his mother's black clothes. Betty might respond by immediately jumping up, shouting at Steve, telling him how inconsiderate he is, and threatening to send him to the hospital again. Steve's retaliation undoubtedly would be further anger, an argument would ensue, and mother and son might end up in a fight.

Consider, instead, the following response. Betty feels furious when she discovers her clothes missing. Rather than immediately confronting Steve, she counts slowly to herself until her initial (quite natural) fury subsides. She then approaches Steve and tells him that throwing away her clothes made her quite angry (not that Steve is inconsiderate), that although she loves Steve, such behavior cannot be tolerated.

This sort of strategy is applicable to any situation that provokes your anger. Frequently it will work. Sometimes it will not. Describing your anger at the behavior rather than at the person, however, is far less threatening than shouting or attacking (verbally or physically) the other person.

Another strategy that might be helpful is to train yourself not to exaggerate the severity of events. Frequently, we perceive an event as calamitous when in fact it is simply an inconvenience. For example, Betty might say to herself, "I can't stand that he threw away my clothes" or "I can't stand *him* for throwing away my clothes." As she does so, her stomach will begin to churn, her shoulder muscles will tighten up. In short, she will become furious. The worst part is, she is exaggerating to herself because, indeed, she *can* stand it; she simply does not like it!

However, Betty could say to herself something like, "Oh no, he threw out my best dress. Well, while that's certainly a nuisance and financially costly, I do have the money to replace it. I certainly don't like this, but it's done now and I guess it's not a disaster in my life." If she thought this way she would feel annoyed and concerned, but not furious.

Perhaps you are saying to yourself, "That's ridiculous! Nobody could go through all that reasoning." The fact is, though, that the way we think is as habitual as driving a car on the right side of the road. Old habits can be broken, and new, more satisfying habits can be learned. In the same way that we can learn to drive on the left side of the road if we visit Britain, we can learn to think in ways that produce moderate, tolerable feelings instead of overwhelming fury or remorse. Initially, we will have to be very purposeful in changing our habit. We must pay attention to our thoughts and work to change them. After a while, though, the new habit becomes second nature and we do not need to exert as much energy. A book that explains this strategy more completely is *A New Guide to Rational Living,* by Albert Ellis and Robert A. Harper (Hollywood, Calif.: Wilshire Book Co., 1975).

Yet another tactic that can help you to express your anger appropriately is to think ahead about the possible consequences of your response. Suppose that Betty is so furious that she feels like slapping Steve. If she gives herself some time to think, she realizes that this will only make matters worse. Steve may respond by hitting her or breaking something. Or perhaps he will simply feel hurt and withdraw. In either case Betty's fury will be replaced later by guilt, which will be considerably more difficult to resolve.

Much of the anger that families of the chronically mentally ill will feel is far less focused than that described above. That is, there may not be a clear reason for the anger other than fate or injustice. It is important, therefore, to find some outlets for irritation and frustration lest they turn into more serious anger.

Talking to other people can be quite helpful. Especially valuable in this respect are the support and discussion groups of families of the mentally ill that are springing up throughout the country. Since members of such groups share the difficulties and the stigma of mental illness in the family, they can talk freely with one another. True empathy emerges when, for example, one father tells another about having to walk the streets all night to find his son. Sometimes friends, professionals, or others, such as clergy, can be safe people with whom to share your anger and frustration. Someone outside the family can be especially useful, since there are no repercussions of expressing your anger. It is also important for family members to be engaged in activities other than the those required by the illness. This helps ensure that they do not end up feeling like slaves to the mental illness, with no control over their lives.

6

Other Emotional Effects

The ongoing strain of chronic mental illness often produces a great deal of family conflict. It is true that some families find that the crises and daily work of caring for the chronically mentally ill member pull them closer together. One mother of a schizophrenic girl found that she and her husband "shared more and supported each other more" than any time before their daughter became ill. For other families, family groups or religious organizations provide enough support to help them overcome the potentially disrupting effect of the illness on family relations.

It is, however, far more common for family members to feel at odds with one another. The many pressures of chronic mental illness can work to divide the family. Naturally, families will not feel strained every hour of every day. Nevertheless, conflicts will occur often enough to put serious stress on the family, both as a system and as individuals.

Family Conflict

Whether the illness is schizophrenia, diabetes, or cancer, many families of the chronically ill experience a general increase in tension. Some of this tension may express itself in disagreement about child-rearing styles. How often have you heard parents disagree about child rearing? "You coddle him too much." "I wouldn't have to if you spent more time with him." "Maybe we should give her money to mow the lawn each week." "She shouldn't have to be paid to do her chores." As long as people have children, there will be some disagreement about how best to raise them. When children turn out fine, everyone forgets these differences of opinion, but when something goes wrong, as in the case of chronic mental disability, quite ordinary disagreements about child rearing may be blown up in an attempt to find the culprit.

Although, as we have emphasized, there is no culprit, too much inconsistency among family members can have a negative effect on the ill relative. He may become more confused, "play off" one family member against another, or simply act inconsistently himself.

Here is an example. Steve Lacey is sitting around watching his mother unload the weekly groceries from the car. Betty Lacey has decided that Steve should not be pressured at all. Tom Lacey comes home and finds his son supervising Betty's work. Tom, fully expecting Steve to help out, tries to get Steve to work. Angry words might be exchanged. Betty, through her actions, has already shown that she expects little from Steve. Tom and Betty may then openly disagree about what is best for Steve, while Steve looks on. Soon the discussion shifts to Tom and Betty and their respective treatment and expectations of Steve. What started as an attempt to get Steve to help out has turned into an argument between Betty and Tom.

This scenario is common. Its effects are negative for everyone concerned. Tom and Betty may accuse each other of taking the wrong approach to Steve's problems and of not having Steve's welfare in mind. Feelings invariably are hurt. Family members are driven apart when they should be combining their resources. The ill family member perceives the disagreement and is confused about how to act. Rather than having the structure that is needed, the family finds itself divided and inconsistent.

Clearly, family members cannot and should not always agree. But it is important for family members to *act* consistently, though they may continue to hold different opinions. In the Laceys' case, for example, though Tom and Betty may disagree about their expectations for Steve, they can agree to try a particular approach. Betty might help Tom to set up an agreement with Steve in which helping with groceries is exchanged for rides to town. Tom and Betty must work together to enforce such an agreement, since it cannot be effective if only one of them tries it. If this method does not work well for them, then they can try something else. In short, they may disagree on the ultimate value of expecting Steve to do some chore, but agree to try to modify his behavior. This helps establish the predictability that the mentally ill person needs.

It is important for family members to discuss openly their differences of opinion. They also should evaluate their behavior periodically to see if the problems that had caused them difficulty have been reduced. In all of these discussions, the one thing to avoid is accusation. Chronic mental illness is not easy for anyone. Each family member responds as he thinks best and usually with good intentions. Recognition of each other's feelings and viewpoints will go a long way toward strengthening the family and working out compromises in the treatment of the ill relative.

Many families who must care for an ill relative over a long period of time experience increased irritability, tension, and unease. Sometimes these emotions can be traced directly to the ill person. It is quite natural to be frustrated and irritated when your relative fails to clean his room or to give you an important telephone message.

More difficult to recognize is the general rise in conflict and tension that has no apparent relation to the illness itself. Family members have reported feeling "more irritable. I seem to have a short temper much of the time. Sometimes silly things

set me off, like answering the phone and it's a wrong number."
Other family members may find themselves more critical of
one another. Some people experience a constant background
of tenseness, others experience fleeting moments of irritability.
Whatever its form and intensity, tension is a frequent consequence of constant care and never-ending responsibility.

Role ambiguity further strains family relationships, especially as it becomes clear that the family member is chronically
ill. Because of her frequent periods of confusion and agitation,
a husband must look out for his wife in the same way parents
look out for their child. Has the gas oven been turned on by
accident? Is his wife dressed properly for the weather? Has she
been eating nutritious food? Family members often feel conflict over their roles. Is it "right" to treat a wife "like a child"?
If not, what will happen to the ill member who is not given
this extra protection?

Mental illness not only forces role confusion in the healthy
family members, it also increases the number of roles a family
member must fill. A seventeen-year-old woman responds in
some ways as a daughter to her ill mother, but she also protects
her mother as would a parent. She sees that her mother remembers her medication and takes her mother to the mental health
clinic. She may take on an additional parental role toward her
younger brother and fix his lunch before school, help with his
homework, and help him get ready for bed. She may further
become a confidante for her father, listening to his concerns
in much the same way that his spouse would if she were able
to.

The strain of the demands and behavior of the ill person may
cause healthy family members to drift apart, to fight with one
another over the ill member, and to generally become more
isolated. The splitting up of the family into individuals struggling with one another further increases the burdens of chronic
care. Sometimes the tension and divisiveness become so great
that family members may separate and divorce. The parents of
a schizophrenic daughter divorce after twenty-five years of

marriage. The daughter-in-law of a chronically ill man leaves her husband because she can no longer bear the unpredictability of the illness and the strain on her marriage. Sometimes divorces are precipitated in the midst of emotional upset. Other times it seems as if all avenues have been explored and the couple simply can no longer live together—the marital relationship has been put under too much stress. Exploration, perhaps with a professional, of the specific issues causing stress in the relationship may help couples deal with their differences in more mutually supportive ways.

Physical Symptoms of Stress

Many families have reported the development or intensification of physical problems and have linked their problems to the stress of chronic care. One man complains of regular headaches, something he never had when younger. A mother finds that she has digestive problems that coincide with her son's bizarre behavior. Yet another person reports that a preexisting heart condition seems to worsen during family crises.

Although we do not know for certain that these physical complaints are a direct result of caring for the chronically ill person, there is no doubt that chronic care produces stress. It is quite reasonable to expect some individuals to respond to this stress with physical problems. If you know that you are prone to physical illness when under pressure, you should take special care in minimizing stress as much as possible and obey your body's early warning signs. Some people get an upset stomach or develop headaches, others suffer from stiff muscles and neck aches. Whatever your own response to stress, take time to care for yourself. Many families find physical exercise, such as jogging or bicycling, to be relaxing and an outlet for daily stress. Movement may even deter various physical complaints. Some individuals find meditation relaxing, while others develop hobbies that allow them to focus their attention on something other than their problems. Although some of these activities may be temporarily given up

74

at times of crisis, the family must see to it that this is not a permanent situation.

Finding other ways of reducing stress may take some concerted thought and planning. It may mean taking advantage of the times when your relative is not at home—either for a few hours or for a number of days. If your relative is not working, you may wish to plan for him to be in some sort of day program that will allow you some breathing room. This time should be used constructively. You may wish to devote time to your own work or hobbies. You may want to simply relax, sit down, and read a book. These times are also excellent opportunities for inviting over friends you might not otherwise have the chance to see.

It is also essential for you to plan your own time away. This can mean evenings out, vacations, or perhaps a job. Many relatives report that they give up leisure-time activities because of guilt, lack of time, or embarrassment. Either the ill member does not seem able to handle social situations or the family does not feel sure that the relative can manage at home alone. The restriction on social life insulates the family from others, and it becomes self-absorbed in its own difficulties. Life becomes boring and tedious. Family members lose vital sources of support and rejuvenation.

Many families feel unsure about leaving their relative at home. How do you decide if your relative can manage alone? A useful method is to leave at first for only a short period, perhaps an hour, and be close at hand so that you can return promptly if a difficulty arises. Later you can begin to expand the time and go greater distances, always leaving a number where you can be reached. This gradual process allows both you and your relative to adjust comfortably to your being away. You may both discover that everything runs more smoothly than either of you had anticipated.

No matter what chances for relief you may find, the attention required in the care of your relative is still draining. One mother of a schizophrenic daughter commented:

There are no mental vacations. Even when you are physically away from the ill person, you are thinking about her, "Is she all right? Should I call to check? Did she remember to shut off the stove after cooking dinner? Did she wander out in the middle of the night?"

Another mother said of her chronically ill daughter:

I lie in bed some nights and I shudder thinking about her off in some town being with God knows who and doing God knows what, and I really have to block it right out. I could really freak out some nights thinking about what's happening.

A major effect of the constant mental burden is that family members simply have less to give one another after providing so much emotionally for their relative. Even the most well-adjusted family members can feel hurt and resentful about this lack of attention to their own concerns.

In order to correct the situation, some families purposefully set about separating the ill family member from the others. This seems to be particularly true of parents trying to help their other children. One couple, for example, supported their healthy child's move to another city. They said, "She has her own life to lead. Why should she have to be burdened?" Other families make sure that there are chances for the healthy members to do things without the chronically ill person.

Another reason for separating family members is to facilitate the ill member's adjustment. Some families feel that there is more to be gained by reducing the family pressures on the ill person than by trying to have the person fully integrated into the family.

However well intentioned these attempts to reduce the stress on individual family members are, they can have a serious consequence that is ultimately detrimental. If not used carefully, these family maneuvers can isolate the ill person from his family. One family, for example, made sure that their healthy children's friends visited only when their schizophrenic offspring was out of the house. They encouraged all the healthy children to develop social contacts and activities that excluded the ill sibling. All of this was done to ease the strain on the family, but as a result the ill person was effectively cut off. He felt even less confident about himself and interpreted his family's actions as a sign of shame. It is better for all concerned to strike a balance that allows family members to have their own time and interests as well as do things together. As in any family, there will always be some conflict between individuals and the family unit. However, protection of the individual (whether ill or healthy) must not be bought at the cost of isolation. It may often seem easier in the short term to reduce conflict by keeping family members away from one another, but the long-term effect is to drive the family apart. This division serves only to increase the withdrawal of the ill person. The ill person is told, in effect, that he cannot be a part of the family.

Some compromises are possible that allow for attention to both the ill member's needs and those of the well family members. For instance, many families have mixed feelings about holiday times when their relative is in the hospital. Should they have their relative home and risk a tumultuous holiday at the expense of everyone's enjoyment? Or should they leave their relative in the hospital, only to feel guilty and concerned about the ill member being alone at such a time? A choice that could be made is to have the ill person home for one day over a three-day holiday period. In that way the entire family has the opportunity to be together for some time, and the well family members leave themselves the chance to relax, free from supervising and being on guard.

In making these choices the family members can remind themselves that they will be ineffective caretakers if they do not also care for themselves and take some time out.

Stigma and Shame
The social aspects of caring for your ill relative include decisions regarding whom to tell, how to tell others, and facing

the reactions of family, friends, and the general public. As much as families might fantasize about avoiding unfeeling or uncaring outsiders, it is impossible to completely prevent these encounters. Furthermore, "hiding" mental illness simply isolates the ill relative and his family even more and helps to maintain social stigma.

Telling people that you have a mentally ill relative is a very difficult task in our society. Many persons view mental illness as a demonstration of inadequate parents or "sick" families. Therefore, to tell someone, even another member of the family, that your spouse, child, or parent is mentally ill is to risk social criticism. After all, who wants to "admit" to something that may cause others to see you as a failure or even as a "bad" person?

Many family members find that they also have unthinkingly held these beliefs. That is, many families report that before mental illness was apparent in their relative, they believed that serious mental disorders were a direct result of family rearing or poor family relations. Thus, these family members felt poorly about themselves and thought they were failures because they believed in these cultural myths. It is the rare family indeed that has not experienced some embarrassment or shame, most especially during the early stages of the illness. While these are common and reasonable feelings in light of the social climate and beliefs, families need not be trapped by these feelings. We have repeatedly emphasized that families do not specifically cause serious psychiatric disorder, so there is no real reason for them to feel like failures or bad people. Nevertheless, it will continue to be difficult to discuss mental illness with others until there is a general shift in public attitudes.

Once you have successfully overcome your own initial emotional responses, should you tell others? The best way to handle this is to act openly and matter-of-factly. While family members need not go out of their way to tell people about their mentally ill relative, they should not hide the fact, either. When friends who had not seen Karen in a while asked Sue and Dan how she was doing, they responded, "She had been having some problems in her life, became ill, and is currently being treated at the state hospital. It has been a difficult time for all of us."

You should recognize that even your best efforts may not always meet with success. There is always a social risk in revealing the existence of mental illness. People are often startled, embarrassed, or simply confused about how to respond. They frequently will avoid the subject altogether. Says one relative:

> I noticed people wouldn't speak about her . . . People would often ask about the family, and those who know about her would never ask how she was doing. People are very hesitant about that kind of thing . . . They feel maybe they are prying into your business. Even the helping people don't know how to help. There was a point there when just a little interest or a word would have been helpful . . . People don't know how to do it.

As Betty Lacey had said, "I think people don't ask because they think they're going to hurt you by asking."

Perhaps most difficult for families to understand and accept is the failure of the extended family to support them. Sisters, brothers, cousins, and others who previously had been close and supportive no longer call, come over, or help out. As one family member observed, "The rest of the family can't seem to keep any contact." Parents of the chronically mentally ill often find that their healthy children no longer remain in touch with the family once they have left home and established their own lives. Some family members may not be able to devote the time and energy to the care of their ill relative that others may. If their need to have some emotional and even physical distance from the situation is recognized, they may still be able to provide some support without being closely involved.

The overall effect of societal attitudes upon families is to leave them feeling abandoned and alone. There is also a good measure of anger expressed by families toward others for failing to provide support. Part of that anger results from the knowledge that had the ill relative been physically rather than mentally sick, there would have been sympathy and support.

There is no way to change this sort of situation overnight. Nevertheless, we do know that family and friends are frequently unsure and embarrassed in the face of mental illness. Mystery and stigma continue to surround it. Sometimes an acknowledgment of others' confusion or embarrassment will provide the necessary permission they need to talk with you. Sue and Dan might say to their friend, "We know it seems awkward sometimes, but it's okay for us to talk about Karen." In cases where people mean well but hurt you, again you can recognize their good intentions, yet point out why it hurts. For example, Betty might reply to a person who suggested locking Steve up for good, "I know you have my best interests in mind, but I'd feel awful locking him up." This type of response is not guaranteed to work. Sometimes others will not really hear you; they may continue to fear mental illness and remain embarrassed and unsure.

By its very nature, chronic mental illness guarantees that there will always be some stress. The pressures and conflicts we have discussed in this chapter will not go away, although they may vary in strength. It is to the family's advantage, therefore, that the nature of stress be understood and steps taken to reduce it when possible. The natural force tending to drive families apart can be counteracted by supporting one another and working in unison rather than as separate individuals. This requires constantly communicating with one another clearly, sympathetically, and cooperatively.

III

YOU AND YOUR RELATIVE DAY BY DAY

7

Understanding
Your Relative's Experience

ऽ

Susan is twenty-eight years old. When she was eighteen and in her first year at college, she began to show signs of severe depression. She became withdrawn, thin, and haggard-looking. She telephoned her priest at all hours of the day and night, asking to make confession, at which point her parents became alarmed and sought treatment.

Initially, the outlook seemed optimistic. Susan was hospitalized for a few weeks and given medication that controlled her disturbed thoughts and alleviated her depression. Both Susan's family and her physician hoped this bright, attractive young woman would be able to resume her activities and achieve her goals.

Susan returned to college feeling that her problems were behind her. She was confident that she could resume her normal activities. Her depression had lifted completely, and in fact she felt so well that she stopped taking her medication. Surely, she thought, she was healthy now, if indeed she ever had been ill. She saw the whole episode as a case of "silly adolescent blues."

Within six months, Susan was back in the hospital. This time the symptoms were different. Gradually she began sleeping poorly and her mood became excessively elated. She felt she could do anything. Thinking she was invisible and could fly, she climbed the dormitory roof stark naked. This time she was in the hospital for three months. Her family was worried and edgy, as was Susan. She knew now that she could never tolerate the embarrassment of going back to that school. But where could she go? And how could she be certain that the same thing would not happen again?

Upon discharge, Susan decided to attend community college while living at home with her family. Although she would have preferred to live away from home, she was becoming frightened of being on her own.

Susan felt out of place at the new school. She had lost a year because of her illness and was out of step with current fads and fashions. She found it hard to start conversations, and she sometimes worried that people would find out that she had been in a mental hospital. The work seemed harder too, although she had expected it to be easier.

Just before final exams, Susan became convinced that the teachers were conspiring to have her thrown out of school for "infecting" the other students with her disease. She became furious and went from office to office accusing and berating the college staff. Frightened and confused, she returned to the hospital voluntarily.

Susan has had six psychiatric hospitalizations in the past ten years. She no longer expects to earn a college degree. Indeed, she would be surprised if she were able to hold a steady job. Having so badly disappointed her family and herself, she appears to have little motivation to set or achieve goals. Her symptoms flare up only occasionally, but she is chronically depressed and withdrawn. Her parents feel as if they were living with a stranger.

Whatever the diagnosis, and regardless of specific symptoms, people with chronic mental illness have a number of common problems and concerns. First, most mental illnesses run relatively unpredictable, intermittent courses, first encouraging and then dashing hopes for recovery. Unable to predict how well he might be able to function at any time in the future, the individual is unable to make plans that carry even a moderate likelihood of success. Second, mental illness is hidden from others in a way that most physical illnesses are not. Thus, the person may constantly fail to meet the expectations of others for no *apparent* reason. Third, mental illness is a stigmatizing condition. The support and encouragement afforded to the person with a chronic physical disability are often unavailable to the mentally disabled individual. In this chapter we use Susan's experiences to illustrate the feelings common to individuals with chronic mental illness and the effects of those feelings upon other members of the family.

The process of accepting and adjusting to chronic illness of any kind occurs gradually in both the sufferer and the family. Uncertainty, hope, anger, depression, and despair emerge and recede many times before a relatively stable adaptation is found.

Typically, one acute episode of mental illness is not sufficient to cause either the disturbed individual or the family to reevaluate its goals. After a period of uncertainty, the crisis ebbs and the pieces of life begin to fit together as before. This is as it should be, since some people do indeed have a single "nervous breakdown" of some kind and appear to recover completely. Further, the specter of chronic mental illness is such a catastrophic one that avoidance is natural. So even an unrealistically hopeful attitude is quite normal at this point. It is only after multiple episodes that most people begin to accept the fact that they have a chronic disability.

Susan's second hospitalization brought her face-to-face with the question of whether or not she was "sick." Brought to the hospital by ambulance, she was confined to a locked unit, given medication, and expected to be quiet and cooperative. The staff continuously urged her to calm herself and to rest. But Susan did not feel sick. Indeed, she felt superbly, unnaturally healthy. Quickly, her confusion gave way to rage. How dare her family confine her against her will? They were crazy, not she! When they visited, she screamed, cried, and pleaded to be released. She threatened to sue them, to hate them, and to disown them. Between visits, she treated the nurses and doctors contemptuously. She was withdrawn, sullen, and uncooperative.

Most families, like Susan's, feel devastated by their relatives' angry responses to treatment. Indeed, many times a family will fail to seek help for its disturbed relative because it cannot bear to face the accusations it knows will follow. Some have removed their disturbed relatives from treatment facilities too quickly because they have felt so guilty.

It helps to keep in mind that anger and resentment are natural responses to the circumstances in which your relative finds himself. It does not necessarily mean that the illness is getting worse. Neither does it mean that the family has erred in seeking treatment. Rather, it is a way of coming to grips with the idea of chronic illness. As the individual regains contact with reality, anger is frequently replaced by shame and self-deprecation. Anger at family members may reemerge from time to time, but it rarely remains the sole way in which the individual responds.

How can you deal with the disturbed individual who blames you inappropriately, who accuses you of trying to "put me away," or "hold me back"? Rather than simply denying the person's perceptions, you would do better to respond reflectively and with concern. This is more easily accomplished if you can learn to focus your attention on how your disturbed family member is feeling rather than on your own feelings of uncertainty or guilt. Consider, for example, the following response to Susan's anger:

We didn't want to put you in the hospital. We didn't know what else to do. How could you say we don't love you? You know that's not true. We would do anything for you!

While all of these statements are undoubtedly true, they are unlikely to satisfy Susan (although they may help the well family member to feel less guilty). Probably Susan will continue to feel as if no one understands or cares about her feelings, only about their own. An alternative might be,

I can see you're really angry, and I guess I would be too if I felt that somebody I trusted was locking me up against my will. We must seem awfully heartless to you right now.

Accepting a person's anger as understandable generally will help dissipate it. Putting yourself, for the moment, in your relative's shoes can help you do this effectively. Asking your disturbed family member to stand in your shoes, as in the first response, is typically asking too much.

By the time she was recovering from her second acute episode, Susan was becoming aware that her behavior immediately preceding her hospitalizations had been bizarre by all normal standards. Coping with shame can be a major problem for people who are recovering from an acute episode in which their behavior was socially inappropriate or aggressive. Having done awful things, they perceive themselves to be awful people. They wonder how they will ever be able to redeem themselves in the eyes of others or in their own eyes. Families can help their relatives gain some perspective by gently emphasizing a few points.

First, we have all embarrassed ourselves badly and lived to talk about it. Perhaps you could share with your relative one of your own most embarrassing moments. If the behavior occurred among strangers, you can remind your relative that most likely he will not have to face them again, and in any case their opinion of him cannot affect him greatly. If the observers were family or friends, they probably are willing to forgive, if not forget, his behavior.

You can also help your relative attribute certain behaviors to his illness rather than to his intentions. For example, Susan's parents can reassure her that she is not a "shameless tramp" because of her public nudity. She wasn't "thinking straight" then, nor was she "in touch with reality." The individual must learn to separate the sick self from the healthy self. At the same time, he must understand that he has some control over the appearance of symptoms in his decision to cooperate or not with treatment and in his setting realistic goals. While you may heartily disapprove of the disturbed and disturbing behavior, you can still accept your relative as a person and support him in looking ahead instead of focusing on the past.

Susan's emotional responses to her problems also were changing. Although after the first episode she was confident and hopeful, now she was frightened and confused. Anger at her parents was mild and short-lived. Now she actively sought their support. Indeed, she seemed distressed when required to make any decisions at all. She was also easily disarmed by any criticism, however slight. She seemed to have lost all of her self-confidence. She wondered aloud how anybody could still love her after what she had done. She felt like a fool.

Uncertain how control over her behavior had slipped from her grasp, Susan adopted an attitude of constant watchfulness. She developed a heightened self-consciousness, mercilessly scrutinizing her actions against a perfectionistic standard. For example, having behaved "indecently" when she was ill, Susan was extremely careful to dress primly and to refrain from the use of coarse language. She avoided doing anything that might be considered flirtatious or sexy. She rarely smiled at people she did not know, and never at young men in any case. Indeed, her behavior was so correct, so uncompromising, that other students at the community college found themselves uncomfortable in her presence. Having sacrificed spontaneity for control, Susan seemed unable to "loosen up."

This fear of losing control and the related sense of having to "walk on eggshells" to be extremely careful not to "crack" again are common among people recovering from an acute emotional breakdown. Since the maintenance of such rigid control is very tiring, the person may become much less outgoing and effervescent than he or she once was. People close to the individual usually recognize the change and rarely like it. The person may seem devoid of feeling, like a·robot. The family's initial response may be to tell the person to relax, to pressure the person to liven up or behave more spontaneously. In other cases the family may also begin to walk on eggshells, attempting not to upset or disturb the individual.

Neither the false sense of gaiety of the former strategy nor the gloom of the latter is of much help to the family. You can help most by understanding that your relative *must* learn to monitor and evaluate his behavior, even if it means sacrificing some spontaneity. Indeed, you can help him do so by providing feedback when asked and by allowing him to retreat to a private place when he needs rest. It rarely helps for the family to curtail drastically the spontaneity of its other members—to do so burdens the ill member with the sense of having deprived others of pleasure.

Your relative may be reluctant to join the family in activities for fear of acting badly, or he may be overly dependent on the family's reassurance. For example, he may no longer be willing to shop for clothes, take public transportation, or go to a party without being accompanied by a member of the family. This is a point at which counter-productive patterns can easily be set in motion if you begin to behave as if your relative has become a child again. While you can and should empathize with your relative's fearfulness, you ought to encourage independent behavior. This can be a very difficult period for the well family members who observe their disturbed member's uncertainty and anxiety but feel they are unable to help. Unfortunately, such a period often ends with yet another episode of disturbance, reinforcing everyone's sense of helplessness. So it was with Susan.

Following her third hospitalization, Susan began to develop a sense of helplessness that was to become more profound with each successive failure. Over time, her motivation to pick up the pieces and begin again became weaker and weaker. She knew that she had disappointed and hurt her family. She knew that she was unable to ensure that it would not happen again. She could sense that those around her had given up on her, that they no longer expected her to achieve her goals. While she was relieved that they no longer pressured her, she felt unsupported and even abandoned. Gradually she withdrew from her family as she had withdrawn from her peers. She did not want to see the concern, the fear, and the hurt in their faces. Occasionally she lashed out at them, blaming her parents once again for her failures or blaming a hostile, unforgiving society. Mostly she blamed herself.

The individual who finally faces long-term impairment often becomes depressed and despairing. He now carries the burden of many failures: He has been unable to conquer the problem alone; he has caused his family pain and financial cost; he has failed to achieve personal and social goals; he has been ostracized by his peers. He is unable to find a really satisfactory explanation for his failures. The person who finds himself unable to control antisocial, inappropriate, or incompetent behavior frequently sees himself as evil, stupid, or even worthless.

He carries this burden into new social situations and into job interviews. Sorely lacking in self-confidence, he worries about other people's perceptions of him. Furthermore, he has reason to worry—surveys indicate that most people do fear, dislike, and expect the worst of people who they know are mentally ill. Rather than face telling a prospective employer or new acquaintance about his illness, he may avoid these situations. Or, feeling that he will betray himself by some unplanned word or deed, he may defensively blurt out that he has mental problems long before the relationship calls for this disclosure. In any case, social anxiety frequently creates the kinds of problems the person most seeks to avoid.

You may be tempted to paint a rosy picture of the future in order to help your relative feel more comfortable; however, we would advise against it. For example, if you blithely assure your relative that a prospective employer will "understand" about his psychiatric history, you risk setting him up for an unanticipated rejection or setting yourself up as a useless source of advice. Instead, you can counsel him that some businessmen will give him a chance, but others will not. The reality is that he may have to go through a larger number of job interviews than other people in order to get a job, but the prospect is not totally bleak. When he tells you that a friend with whom he has shared information about himself is now more reserved and distant, do not immediately assume that he is being overly sensitive. It may be, instead, that you are being naïve. But if he tells you that he feels worthless because of the friend's response (or the prospective employer's rejection), you can remind him that prejudice reflects on those who have it, not on those against whom it is directed.

Nonetheless, despite what you may tell him about the possibility of future successes, your relative is functioning against a backdrop of multiple failures. He has seen firsthand the vacant stares of the chronically institutionalized patients, and each successive rehospitalization decreases his expectation that he will escape their fate.

Many people, like Susan, simply give up at some point. Their expectation of success is so small that they are unwilling to risk additional failures. Giving up can take many forms. Some people refuse to stay on medication, preferring the excitement and variety of their fantasy life to the drab, dull pain of reality. Others become institutionalized, preferring the nonstressful environment of the hospital to the demands of the outside world (although hospitals are less and less willing to keep such people, and sheltered living circumstances in the community are rare). Most simply withdraw, exhibiting no initiative and interacting little. Such a solution is painful for the family, but it is understandable from the ill person's point of view.

In contrast to those who give up, some people never seem to face the chronicity of their illness. This is called denial and represents one natural way in which people unconsciously protect themselves from painful revelations. It occurs commonly among people with life-threatening illnesses, such as cancer ("The diagnosis must be wrong" or "They'll be able to cure my illness"), and other disabilities, including mental illness. Denial may also be employed during painful life circumstances, such as divorce or death of a close family member or friend. Most people do get over it in time and move toward a more realistic appraisal of their situation.

However, when denial involves dangerous or irresponsible behavior, such as stopping needed medicine, the family is placed on the horns of a dilemma. It seems as if confronting the denial directly causes friction and stress, while ignoring it is irresponsible and callous. There are two possible approaches that might be helpful. The first is to help your relative become aware of the fear that is behind the denial, again using reflective responses. For example, you might say,

> I know that taking medicine makes you feel as if what is happening is beyond your control. It must be pretty scary to think that this is a sickness that you can't do anything about.

Such a response, while not a magic cure, may help your relative take one small step toward a more realistic appraisal of the situation.

An alternative, useful in cases where denial really interferes with progress, is the "steam-roller" approach:

> I know you don't think you're sick, but you must take your medicine if you're going to live at home.

Obviously, this approach engenders a degree of resentment and should be used sparingly.

Some people cope with the chronicity of their illness by continuing to struggle to be normal, although with realistically reduced goals. These people generally cooperate with treatment, persist in acquiring social skills, and actively seek support and guidance. However, even they experience a certain amount of discomfort and depression. Like Susan, they may continue to feel out of step with their peers. Many feel most comfortable with people younger than they are, from whom the social demands are more consistent with what they were able to learn between bouts of acute illness. They have had to give up goals that they might have accomplished had they not become ill. They have also sacrificed much of the anticipatory pleasure with which most of us face the future. In short, they mourn what might have been while accepting what is.

The family cannot ensure that its disturbed member will follow the latter course. Much depends on the intellectual and emotional resources upon which the person can call. Another factor is whether the person's fantasy life is pleasant and compelling or frightening and painful. A person who feels able to control other people when psychotic is less likely to comply with treatment than one who feels hunted by invisible enemies.

Of great importance is the discrepancy between the person's potential before and after his illness. For example, a successful engineer found that he could not tolerate the stress of his occupation following his breakdown. He had to accept a less responsible job. Someone like this may lose hope more quickly than a person who might not have had the same high expectations originally. In general, the larger the gap, the more painful and difficult will be the adjustment. However, you can provide emotional support, understanding, and opportunities for successes that may make reality appear somewhat more worthwhile to your relative.

Mental illness, by its very nature, frequently precludes your relative's ability to understand himself or his situation fully. Judgment is impaired; reality testing is impaired; emotional responsiveness is impaired. Thus, accepting that one has a chronic mental illness can be a painful, lengthy, and often incomplete process. Each person approaches the problem in a unique way and each will find his own final adaptation. Anger at family members, refusal to take medication, and avoidance of work are all frustratingly common aspects of this process. Just as many diabetics resent and rebel against their dietary restrictions and their lifetime need for medication, so do many mentally ill individuals resist treatment suggestions. Family members who can supportively communicate understanding of what their disturbed relative experiences can be a valuable resource.

8

Providing a
Therapeutic Environment

Living with a chronically ill relative is at best difficult. Many times you will regret the decision to keep your relative at home and feel trapped in an impossible situation. However, specific goals and guidelines toward which you can work will directly influence day-to-day disruptions and make it easier for everyone to cope. Family life can be more settled and rewarding if family members feel more in command of their daily existence. This chapter offers some suggestions for providing more effectively for the disturbed relative living at home.

It is not, however, a forgone conclusion that your relative will live at home. This is a decision that must be mutually agreed upon by all members of your family, taking into consideration the needs of the well members as well as those of the ill person. We shall discuss this decision in more detail in Chapter 12. Nevertheless, many of the suggestions and observations made in this chapter can also be used by the family that does not have full-time responsibility, but whose relative lives nearby and with whom it is actively involved.

Reducing Stress

Stress means different things to different people. We all experience stress daily—a hard day at work, an argument with our spouse, or a new refrigerator breaking down. Stress may also be more general and long-lasting. We may be concerned about inflation, holding our job, and crime in the neighborhood. Any situation that requires us to change or adapt can be stressful, even positive experiences, such as the birth of a child or grandchild. Most of us are able to tolerate some stress and continue to manage our everyday affairs.

For the mentally ill individual, many of the decisions involved in daily living, such as what to cook for breakfast or how to dress for dinner, can cause stress. More general concerns, such as looking for a job or going out on a date, can create additional tension. Stress is often disruptive to the daily functioning of the mentally ill person. The concern over what to cook for breakfast may be so immobilizing that no breakfast is made at all. Considerable stress can lead to an increase or renewal of psychiatric symptoms.

Since stress is a factor in relapse, excessive stress is neither therapeutic for the individual nor comfortable for the family. It can lead to a deterioration in logical and coherent thinking, and it can cause a disruption in the ill relative's ability to function and in the family's ability to cope with even daily routine matters.

The first step in providing a low-stress environment is to be more supportive of the ill member, keeping criticism and negative remarks to a minimum. Research has shown a significant correlation between relapse of the patient and a highly emotionally charged family environment. A supportive atmosphere will reduce the individual's symptoms and the overall tension level within the family. This does not mean that you must constantly keep your emotions pent up inside you and avoid arguments twenty-four hours a day. This would be unrealistic as well as damaging to everyone's emotional well-being. It does mean, however, that you can work toward calmer and more controlled displays of emotion. Your family may find that with some added thought and patience, they can avoid unnecessary and tension-producing arguments. If the ill person wishes to cook a meal but leaves the kitchen messy and cluttered, you can try to appreciate the effort and refrain from commenting on the clean-up problem. In this way you can save your emotional energies for more momentous problems and crises.

As a family you may also need to lessen your demand for support from your ill relative. A wife may find that her ill husband, who needs to use all of his energies simply to get from day to day, can no longer provide a sounding board for her problems. She may need to seek emotional support from other relatives, friends, or professionals.

A supportive atmosphere should be accompanied by limit-setting and structure. A chronically ill individual is usually coping with confused thoughts and emotions. He needs a routine to add a degree of order and calm to an otherwise tumultuous state. Chronic mental illness also affects the individual's ability to plan daily activities, particularly if he has been hospitalized for any period of time and has become accustomed to the hospital routine. You can provide a structure that initially approximates that of the hospital, gradually stepping back as your relative becomes increasingly able to establish a routine independently. You can be particularly helpful by working out a daily agenda with the person before he leaves the hospital. Activities should occupy time, involve some responsibility, and be enjoyable. If the ill member has a job, you can help with attendance at the job, providing encouragement and incentive. One young woman had tremendous difficulty each morning persuading herself to attend work, but when she got there, she found it rewarding and gratifying. She appreciated her family's firm but gentle push. If the individual does not have a job, there are other programs, such as sheltered workshops, day hospitals, and vocational training, that will provide structure and situations in which he is able to experience increased self-esteem.

Limit-setting also reduces the number of decisions an individual is required to make. Since deciding what to cook for breakfast might be stressful, another family member might help plan the menu and the ill individual can assist in cooking. Decision-making can become gradually more involved as the individual gains self-confidence and indicates that choices are no longer quite so stressful.

Also, try to use various self-control techniques at times of acute stress. When an argument seems likely, taking a deep breath, leaving the room, or sitting down and reading a magazine may sufficiently interrupt the building tension to immediately ease a potentially explosive situation.

Residual Symptoms

Let us now return to Sue and Dan. Karen has spent one year at the state hospital and has shown considerable improvement. She no longer exhibits any violent or self-destructive behaviors. Her thoughts are generally logical and coherent, and her attention span has improved. She has even been able to attend a work program daily. She is on a regimen of psychiatric medication and has apparently accepted her need to continue to take this medication once she leaves the hospital. The treatment team at the hospital decides that Karen is ready to go home.

Sue and Dan are somewhat surprised at this announcement, since there are still some indications that Karen is "not the same young woman she used to be." She still hears voices from time to time, her moods are quite variable, and she has occasional crying spells and sporadic temper outbursts. She also seems easily distracted at times and restless.

Families commonly expect that hospitalization or medication will cure their disturbed relative and that everything will return to normal once the person is ready to return home. In fact, there is frequently a considerable disparity between the individual's readiness to come home and a complete remission of the symptoms. A person may have achieved maximum benefit from hospitalization and no longer require institutional care, but may still have some progress to make before a full remission is achieved. Furthermore, even those whose major symptoms are no longer present may exhibit many signs of chronic illness and may never return to exactly the same condition they were in prior to the onset of psychosis.

Chronic mental illness is not an infection that can be eliminated with antibiotic treatment; it is a condition associated with a wide variety of residual symptoms. Some of the following symptoms may remain, although certainly not in all cases: paranoid thinking, mood changes, inept social behavior, difficulty in concentration, and a tendency to withdraw. Families are often surprised by these residual symptoms and may feel dismayed at the prospect of their long-term presence. Many families feel frustrated when their relatives do not achieve goals even when they appear to be in a good state of remission. Appearances may be deceiving, however, as problems like disrupted thinking and shattered self-esteem may not be readily apparent. The individual, who may have planned further education or vocational training, has had to learn either to reshape his goals according to his current abilities and tolerance for stress or to pursue these objectives more gradually. The family must also try to accept these changes in goals and help their relative experience successful plans rather than repeated failures. You must learn to readjust your expectations of your relative's behavior and goals.

One of the most important ways to proceed is to plan short-term rather than long-term goals. For example, if Karen had intended to enter college before becoming acutely ill, she might continue to head in that direction but begin with only one course. She can then ascertain how easily she can handle schoolwork while not immersing herself in a stressful situation. Vocational counselors and psychologists may be particularly helpful in the administration of some tests that will measure both abilities and interest to give some guidance in selecting appropriate directions.

While helping your relative modify his goals, be careful not to deflate every unrealistic dream. All of us maintain fantasies about who we may become or what we may attain in some vague future. The chronically ill person is no different in the need to have some hopes even if they may be unattainable. As long as these "fantasies" are not the sole guidelines for goal-setting, they will not be destructive.

Families may feel that they are treading a fine line between supporting their ill relatives' pursuits and serving as advocates for realistic goals. They may at times feel that they are holding them back, that perhaps more could be achieved if some of the constraints were removed. It is generally the case, however, that the individual who is able to achieve more will demonstrate that clearly by handling more difficult and complex tasks. Some people achieve more than they themselves, their families, or mental health practitioners have expected. When they are ready, they simply progress. There is significantly more danger in pushing the person too hard and demanding too much than in pushing and demanding too little. This becomes frustrating for both the disturbed member and the family, often leading to failure and relapse.

There are some chronically ill individuals who have become accustomed to doing little with their time and taking little initiative in formulating any plans for the future. In these instances, families can provide encouragement and incentive. This should be a gradual process so that the ill member does not feel pressured into overly stressful achievement-oriented situations. At the same time the person's successful completion of small goals will greatly increase self-esteem and fuel self-confidence.

In the process of appropriate goal-setting, both the individual and the family may wish to reconsider their definition of achievement. Completing a single course or holding a job for six months should be viewed as success and not as something less than the original goal and therefore unsatisfactory.

Realistic Expectations

The preceding sections have dealt with your family's need to modify its expectations and goals and to provide a supportive atmosphere. What can your family expect, then, *from* your relative?

Family members frequently ask how they can distinguish "normal" from "ill" behaviors and which behaviors are within the ill person's control. They are often afraid to make any demands on their relative because they feel that he is unable to control any aspect of his behavior. Conversely, the family may feel that much or all of their relative's behavior is manipulative and may thereby expect that all annoying behaviors should cease. One mother commented on the seeming contradictions in her daughter's attention span and memory:

> She could sit and listen to the radio, a brand-new song, and I wouldn't even be able to understand the words, but she could know it by heart. She would have the words down. And then you'd say, "Would you make your bed," or "Would you do this," and she'd say "Okay" and then she'd get up and say, "What did you ask me to do?"

Mental health professionals often have as much difficulty as families in making distinctions between "normal" and "ill" behavior. For instance, lack of motivation is a common residual symptom of schizophrenia; on the other hand, a person who has been hospitalized for a time may have lapsed into an acquired *habit* of inactivity. Although there is a distinction in the origin of this lack of drive, there need not be a difference in the family's approach to this situation. To find out how well your relative can control his behavior is a matter of trial and error. By asking him to discontinue various behaviors and by rewarding desired behavior, you will learn whether or not he has the ability to control the behavior.

It must be reemphasized that you cannot expect to change all your relative's symptoms or all his irritating behaviors. You must match your family's priorities with the individual's abilities. Keep in mind that you are dealing with a chronic illness that is, in some ways, little different from a long-term physical disability. The person will always require extra care, tolerance, and patience. At the same time this does not mean that life must be chaotic for the rest of the family.

One option is to work out a "behavioral contract," making clear to all concerned what sort of behaviors are acceptable in order for the ill individual to continue living at home. For instance, the ill person may feel unmotivated to pay close attention to his grooming or to household chores. You can clarify your expectations for personal appearance (for example, a shower once per day, clean clothes, neat hair) and tell your relative that he is expected to adhere to these standards equally with the other family members. He should not be excluded from the family division of labor, but he may need to have a more concrete definition of tasks than other members of the family.

The illustration on page 108 is an example of a behavioral contract between Karen and her parents. The tasks listed across the top are Karen's responsibilities. The numbers listed below the tasks indicate the number of points attainable each day if the task is successfully completed. These points should be filled in daily as each task is accomplished. The first three tasks listed are those that Sue and Dan feel are fundamental to Karen's living at home. Personal hygiene and cleanliness are the minimal requirements for their continuing to provide the basic comforts of living at home, such as three meals per day, laundry, cleaning, and access to television. The next three tasks listed are desirable but not necessary. The points assigned to each task are weighted according to their importance, so the first three items are each assigned more points (4) than the three "extras." At the end of each week the points are totaled and Karen is rewarded accordingly. If Karen is able to accomplish more of the tasks than the bare minimum, she receives a carton of cigarettes, and if she is even more industrious, she is taken on a shopping trip over the weekend. If she does not meet the higher point totals, she does not receive the extra rewards. If she does not meet the minimum goal, Sue and Dan are prepared to search for other living arrangements for their daughter.

A behavioral contract is formulated with certain principles in mind: The tasks or goals should be concrete, reachable, and short-term, or the contract will be doomed to failure. It will also fail if rewards and punishments are not given exactly as the contract stipulates. Idle threats will not work. The contract should be extremely clear and both parties should have a good understanding of each part. The points assigned to each task should be weighted according to the importance of the task. The expectation for achievement should allow for occasional backsliding and errors. An individual cannot be expected to accomplish all the expected tasks every single day.

Be sure to set up the contract with as much input as possible from the ill individual, who will know exactly what rewards are appealing. Furthermore, the ill person may have personal goals or tasks that he may wish to add to the contract in addition to the expectations of the well family members.

Requests for behavior change should always be as specific as possible. "We expect you to feed and walk your dog" is much preferable to "It's your dog. Why don't you behave responsibly?" Keep in mind that a focus on your relative's failures will make subsequent failure more likely. Lecturing and nagging produce lots of tension but little positive change.

Finally, a behavioral contract requires a periodic reassessment. As some of the goals become consistently attained and habitual, they should be decreased in importance or replaced by new goals. This reassessment may take place monthly or more often if necessary. Again, participation and input from the ill member should be encouraged. The particular tasks and rewards will vary from family to family. For instance, the ill member may use a lot of profanity. In this case the family may set as a goal the reduction or elimination of the use of profanity. As a middle-level reward, the individual may prefer some extra spending money.

The use of a behavioral contract may require some sacrifice. You may have to reduce some of your expectations in order to ensure cooperation with your most important concerns; likewise, the ill member may have to conform to some rules with which he does not agree, simply because he is living with other people. For example, Sue and Dan wanted Karen to observe the following rules: personal hygiene, room cleanliness, daily household tasks, letting them know her whereabouts. It may be that Karen cannot cooperate with all of these requirements at once. In that case Sue and Dan will have to establish which of these concerns have priority and perhaps relax the demand for daily household tasks in exchange for fulfillment of the other expectations.

You may feel, as one woman did, that establishing rules and definite behavioral guidelines is cruel or "asking too much" of an ill individual:

> There were times when I would get into bed at night and think, "You have to be a heartless, nasty person. How can you be like this with a helpless child? . . . What kind of mother are you?"

Or you may feel that it is simpler not to make these demands:

> [My wife] would come home loaded down with groceries, so I'd go out to help her, and he'd just be sitting there doing nothing.

I'd say to [her], "We're treating him like an invalid." But to get
him to do these things he was capable of doing was an effort.
It was much easier for me to go out and help.

Families are also sometimes reluctant to ask for behavioral
change because it seems that the time is inappropriate to begin
such a discussion. If the ill member is agitated, such a discussion is impossible. If things are going smoothly, families do not
want to bring up topics that might be tension-provoking. One
family talks about the refusal of their daughter to help in any
way with certain household chores and her tremendous agitation if anyone asked her participation: "Just to keep peace in
the family we would go along with it."

You should remember, however, that the central goal in
providing for the ill member at home is to help him adopt as
normal a routine as possible. Structure and defined tasks are
essential in stabilizing a chronically ill person. They help the
family lead a less disruptive and stressful life, but they also help
the ill member function successfully and feel a sense of accomplishment. The ill member's self-esteem is also enhanced if he
feels that the family expects the same things from him that it
expects from other members. A professional may be helpful in
negotiating for this "behavioral contract" reasonable terms
that satisfy the expectations of the family and take into account
the capabilities of the individual.

The family needs to establish some priorities about all behaviors, not just those covered by the behavioral contract. A person
may exhibit a number of behaviors that you consider undesirable. It is unreasonable to expect the elimination of all annoying behaviors, whether they are residual symptoms of the
illness, habitual, or manipulative in nature.

You can be more tolerant of mildly irritating behaviors if
more severely disruptive behaviors are under control. After her
long hospitalization, Karen had developed some habits that
were not acceptable within Sue and Dan's home, such as hasty

and sloppy eating, and frequent napping. These habits were irritating to Sue and Dan, who did not sleep during the day and were accustomed to having a sociable, somewhat protracted dinner hour. Karen had also acquired the habit of dropping ashes from her cigarettes directly on the floor or getting up in the middle of the night and watching television. Sue and Dan could not expect Karen to immediately cease all of these habits. They had to first decide which behaviors were the most disruptive and then engage in a give-and-take with Karen. They had to adjust temporarily to Karen's eating and daytime sleeping habits in exchange for the elimination of the more disruptive practice of nighttime television or the dangerous habit of dropping ashes on the carpet. This sacrifice by Sue and Dan would, in the long run, allow their family life to proceed more smoothly with less tension, which of course would benefit everyone.

When you ask your relative to exert more self-control, you can also encourage more independent behavior. You can help your relative grow by creating opportunities for more adult behavior and be rewarding that behavior when you see it. Fostering self-sufficiency can be difficult when your relative acts confused or helpless or in other ways demonstrates an inability to function independently. The natural response by other family members is to "take over," frequently referred to as "infantilizing" by mental health professionals. As they become accustomed to making decisions and providing guidance, the family may feel or be viewed as if they were treating their relative like an infant.

This infantilizing frequently grows out of the family's confusion about the ill person's ability to function, not its desire for control over the individual. It may be further encouraged by his own insecurities and past failures, which make him reluctant to take risks. However, infantilizing interferes not only with the ill member's attempts at more independence, but also with the family members' freedom as well. The ill person's ability to function, while perhaps severely constricted during a psychotic episode, may return to a near-normal or normal level during a remission, but the family members' expectations may be slow to catch up.

You can promote your relative's self-confidence and independent decision-making, as well as reduce the amount of time and energy that you have been devoting to his care. You can approach this task through a gradual trial-and-error process, slowly increasing the opportunities for independent functioning while assessing your relative's capacities. If, for example, you are worried that your relative cannot negotiate public transportation without getting disoriented or lost, begin by accompanying him on a simple trip. Then have him make the trip alone, and follow this with increasingly more complex trips as long as your relative is doing well.

Be particularly watchful for serious errors in judgment, since this is an area frequently impaired in chronically ill people. These errors may involve money management, choice of friends, or personal safety, to name a few. As you increase your relative's opportunities for independence, you will need to provide extra support for his initially low self-confidence. When the individual begins to make more and more successful decisions, the other family members can gradually step back from the "parenting" role. Some examples of the encouragement of more independent functioning are leaving the person at home alone more often, having the person plan his own excursions, letting him job-hunt, and so on. Remember that you will not always agree with your relative's decisions. Some decisions may even turn out badly, but you and your relative can learn from mistakes. What is important is that your relative be guided toward making more of his own decisions without making gross errors in judgment or experiencing repeated failure.

This trial-and-error process can seem like a painstakingly long one. Remember, however, that the work you invest in providing a supportive, structured environment for your relative can make home life more tolerable and peaceful for everyone.

Behavioral Contract

Tasks and Points

Days of the week	Shower Once Daily	Put on Clean Clothes Daily	Clean Own Room	Clean One Other Room in House	Set Table for Dinner	Cook One Meal	Total
	(4)	(4)	(4)	(3)	(2)	(3)	(20)
Monday							
Tuesday							
Wednesday							
Thursday							
Friday							
Saturday							
Sunday							

65 points weekly = minimum expectation for living at home, receiving meals, having laundry done, watching television

90 points weekly = a carton of cigarettes

115 points weekly = a weekend shopping trip

9

Common Behavior Problems

In Chapter 6 we offered some general strategies for providing a therapeutic environment that would minimize stress while maximizing structure. Creating such an environment depends heavily on your ability to understand and respond constructively to your relative's residual symptoms. It would be impossible to cover every conceivable problem. However, a number of behavioral problems are commonly reported by families with a chronically ill relative, and in this chapter we offer practical advice for coping with some of these.

Social Withdrawal

Most people with chronic mental illness have difficulty in their relations with other people. The severity of the disorder varies widely, from the elderly woman who refuses to leave her room and demands that meals be brought up to her to the young man who appears comfortable with people he knows well but resists, with a thousand excuses, meeting and talking to strangers.

When one member of the family is severely withdrawn or

even socially awkward, rippling effects are felt throughout the family. They may avoid inviting friends and relatives to the house for fear of being embarrassed by their ill relative's withdrawal. Gradually, they may find that they are being invited out less or that they are turning down invitations so as not to leave their relative alone. They begin to feel that they ought to "entertain" the sick family member, but find that their attempts to do so result in disappointingly little success.

Families find their relative's withdrawal burdensome, not only because it impinges on their own lives but also because they are uncertain about what is best for the disturbed family member. Will pushing him into social situations anger and alienate him? Will letting him do as he wishes encourage further isolation? Both are legitimate concerns. Perhaps understanding some of the reasons for social withdrawal will help you make the most helpful choice.

People avoid situations in which they feel anxious or unsure of themselves. People with chronic mental illness often have good reasons for their lack of self-confidence in social situations. First, many of them are well aware that their social behavior has been markedly inappropriate at times in the past when they were highly upset or confused. They may be acutely embarrassed about these episodes and may distrust their ability to prevent a recurrence. This is particularly true of people who continue to experience strange thoughts or feelings. For example, one young man who had spent about twenty minutes in pleasant conversation with his sister became upset and followed her out the door to ask whether he had called her any "bad names" during their conversation. Apparently these bad names had crossed his mind, and he was unsure whether he had uttered them or not. This same young man rarely spoke to anyone who was not a member of his family, and no wonder!

Furthermore, many people whose illness began during adolescence or early adulthood missed the opportunity to learn social skills. Active untreated mental illness prevents the individual from learning these skills by interfering with the ability to think, feel, and behave in a way that is appropriate to the situation. Unfortunately, it is common for such an illness to elude even moderately successful treatment for a number of years. Thus it may happen that a twenty-six-year-old man has had no more successful social experience than a normal sixteen-year-old. Yet he is expected to behave as an adult. Indeed, he shares these expectations with his family and peers, but has little idea of how to accomplish the task. Under these circumstances, the very thought of a social situation may fill him with dread.

To the extent that fear of failure is involved in a person's social withdrawal, what is most needed is to experience success. Avoiding social situations removes the person temporarily from the source of anxiety, but it also removes him from the source of possible rewards. Thus, the greatest danger lies in allowing your relative to become increasingly isolated. It is generally appropriate not only to provide opportunities for social interaction but also to encourage, and in some cases to even insist, that your relative participate.

However, it is most important not to expect too much too soon. Remembering that your ill relative may be frightened and lacking in self-confidence, you can begin by encouraging him to engage in relatively "safe" social interactions. By "safe" we mean asking no more of your relative than he is likely to accomplish successfully. A conversation about the weather is easier to handle than a heart-to-heart talk about feelings. Your family member may be able to handle a chat about sports better than a debate about politics. Brief social interactions are more manageable than extended ones. Usually, family members are safer people to talk with than strangers, if they are able to avoid critical and judgmental remarks.

In deciding what sorts of interactions are "safe" for your relative, you might consider making a list of situations, beginning with those in which he looks most at ease and functions most effectively and ending with those which he appears to avoid. Who are the people your relative responds to best?

What are the topics he feels most comfortable discussing? It may be that the disturbed family member can help compile the list or can develop it himself. In any case, the list can be used to help him progress, in gradual steps, through a variety of social experiences.

It may be necessary to tolerate a certain amount of socially awkward behavior as interaction increases. It is not useful to push your relative into a social situation and then criticize him for embarrassing you. This does not mean that you must tolerate any and all inappropriate behavior. Indeed, if your relative persists in behaving inappropriately in a particular situation, both you and he would be better off if he avoided that situation for a while. But here too, aim for small, gradual improvement, not instant perfection.

Just as it is important to avoid making unrealistic demands, it is useful to remember that rewards will be more effective than punishment. Praise and support work better than nagging and threatening. It may take some time before the pleasures of socializing outweigh the fears. In the meantime, the family's positive responses may help the individual to try again. Even tangible rewards, like a new record or a piece of cake, sometimes can be used to reward appropriate social behavior in a very withdrawn person. The behavioral contract discussed in Chapter 8 can be a useful tool in the development of social skills.

Of course, fear of failure is not the only reason for this social isolation. For some illnesses, schizophrenia in particular, withdrawal is one of the main symptoms, part of the illness itself. Many schizophrenic patients find reality dull and gray compared to the richness and power of fantasy. Others have such a fragile sense of who they are that close relationships with other people are perceived as threatening. Under the right circumstances such threats occur among the rest of us as well. For example, many people find that in the presence of their parents and siblings they act much as they did when they were children. Old grudges, sibling rivalry, and sarcastic interchanges continue, it seems, no matter how old they get. Their image of themselves as mature adults is assaulted and they respond with anger, fear, and often withdrawal. When a person's self-concept has been battered by failures of many kinds, the problem is more acute.

Not all families will meet with the same degree of success in decreasing their relatives' social isolation, but you should proceed under the assumption that significant, although gradual, change is possible. The more systematic your plan and the more supportively you proceed, the greater are your chances of success.

In order to be supportive, the family needs to come to terms with its sense of shame. Frequently the family is as hesitant to resume social life as is the disturbed relative. They are afraid that the ill person will fail again, and they do not want to be embarrassed by his social blunders. They do not want to be the object of other people's pity, surprise, or disgust. These very natural feelings may cause them to support only half-heartedly, if at all, their disturbed member's ventures into the social world. If helping the individual learn to socialize is really a priority for the family, the well members will have to develop a "thick skin."

Lack of Motivation

Social withdrawal is frequently accompanied by general lethargy, apathy, and listlessness. One mother describes her daughter:

> She just sits there smoking cigarettes and staring at the television. She goes nowhere, does nothing. She doesn't care how she looks. She used to play chess really well. . . . Now I don't think she can get through one game.

Families are frequently dismayed by this lack of motivation, a common symptom of chronic mental illness that can take many forms. In some, it may be so severe that the person no longer even pays attention to basic self-care chores, such as bathing, combing hair, brushing teeth, or changing clothes. Others seem slowed down and appear to have lost interest in hobbies or activities. Still others appear to suffer from a lack of initiative or drive. They will participate passively in activities when invited, but fail to seek out projects on their own. In the great majority, the motivation to work is impaired—your relative may work sporadically, irresponsibly, or not at all.

What is actually impaired motivation may look like laziness to the family. Not knowing whether the ill relative is able to control this behavior or not, the family often responds with pushing and cajoling one minute, anger and accusations the next, and apologies at the last. Unhappily, this inconsistency increases the tension the person experiences, thereby further undermining his competence. If, for example, the person is sometimes badgered about personal cleanliness while at other times his appearance is ignored, he may become so confused that he avoids the topic and the family and continues with the behavior.

The listlessness your relative displays may be related to a symptom called "anhedonia," or an inability to experience pleasure. He is probably unable to control how pleasurable things feel: Food just does not taste very good, a party simply is not exciting, an accomplishment does not feel satisfying. It is difficult to work or play or even comb your hair when the satisfaction associated with the activity is missing. For the person with chronic mental illness, much of living may feel like "going through the motions." Yet going through the motions *is* possible, and being willing to do so is a hopeful sign, since it indicates that the individual is motivated to achieve as normal a life style as possible.

You can help with the lethargy in a number of ways. Using the behavioral contract described in Chapter 8 is one good approach. You can also try to provide opportunities for numerous low-stress activities—caring for a pet, riding a bicycle, and gardening, to name a few. Integrate a few such activities into a weekly schedule, and gradually activities that used to feel required and boring may become fun and gratifying. Finally, realize that setting firm but reasonable expectations for your relative's responsibilities for self-care and household chores is appropriate and necessary. The lack of motivation, while very real and very frustrating, can be tackled in a systematic, optimistic way.

Thought Disorder

One of the most common features of chronic mental illness is difficulty in sustained, focused thinking. Your relative may forget instructions with maddening frequency or take what you say more literally than you meant it. He may be unable to stick to a topic of conversation or to understand a joke, read a book, or follow the plot of a movie.

Families are usually able to accommodate themselves to these problems by learning through trial and error what to expect. They can avoid going to the movies with their ill relative altogether, or at least learn to ignore his pacing around the theater lobby. They will learn not to plan unexpected events. A surprise birthday party may delight a healthy family member but disturb the mentally ill member. Although the individual and the family must give up a certain amount of spontaneity, both stand to gain in stability and confidence.

About a third of the people with chronic mental illness experience hallucinations or delusions. A hallucination is a sensory experience in the absence of any real external stimulus —hearing voices when no one is there, for example, or seeing someone who is not there, feeling as if insects are crawling over your body. It can occur in any of the five senses and cannot be controlled by the person experiencing it.

Delusions are false ideas that are not correctable by reason or by the receipt of new information. People who experience delusions of grandeur may believe that they are famous and powerful, that they have a secret cure for the world's problems, or that they can read other people's minds. Delusions of persecution, in which the person feels pursued by evil forces or perceives himself to be the victim of a poisoning plot, can also occur, sometimes simultaneously with delusions of grandeur, as in "I am Jesus Christ and my enemies are persecuting me."

While antipsychotic medication is often highly effective in the reduction or elimination of hallucinations and delusions, many chronic mental patients experience flare-ups of these symptoms when they are under stress. Others continue to experience them continuously, although often at a markedly less disruptive level. These symptoms, hallmarks of mental illness in the minds of the public and professionals alike, are frightening, embarrassing, and provoking for the family. Should you humor your relative? Agree with the bizarre ideas? Try to talk him out of them? Ignore him when he talks about them?

Although a person who experiences delusional ideas or hallucinations cannot be talked out of having them, he frequently can be helped to see that they do not represent reality and ought not to be acted upon. For example, a person who hears voices that tell her to hurt herself can learn to ignore the message even though she cannot stop hearing the voices. She can also learn not to talk about the voices with other people. The ability to distinguish these symptoms from reality varies from individual to individual but generally decreases during periods of acute upset and increases during periods of relative calm.

The family can play an important role in helping the individual handle his loss of contact with reality. Except when your relative is extremely agitated or confused, it *is* appropriate to let him know that the voices are not real, that you are not trying to poison him, that no one can read his mind—*if* you can do it in a constructive way.

Do not get into an argument about whether the ideas are true or false. Paying undue attention to your relative's odd ideas makes it more likely that he will continue to talk about them.

In addition, a stressful argument will provoke increasingly disorganized thinking. A brief, nonemotional statement about reality generally will have the best effect.

Do not laugh at your relative or treat the ideas as if they were jokes. They are not jokes to him, nor is he stupid for having them. Although you will need to deny the validity of his perceptions, it is important to convey respect for him as a person.

Acknowledge the reality of your relative's subjective experiences. Communicate that you understand what he believes and how he feels before you attempt to correct his perception. This helps him accept the correction, whereas a flat denial may cause him to feel confused or angry. For example, a young woman, waiting in line for a movie with her sister, says, "I can't stay here. They're all looking at me. I hate when they all talk about me that way!"

Nonhelpful response: Silence.

Nonhelpful response: "Don't be ridiculous! You know they're not talking about you."

Nonhelpful response: "They're all looking at you because you look so pretty today."

Helpful response: "I know you feel uncomfortable in a group of people, but you look fine and I don't think anyone's talking about you."

Helpful response: "It must be upsetting to feel as though people are always talking about you. I don't think they are, though."

A man is lighting cigarettes and points with them at various objects around the room. When his wife asks why, he replies, "The voices are telling me to."

Nonhelpful response: "What voices? Nobody's here!"

Nonhelpful response: "Oh boy, more crazy talk. Stop it now!"

Nonhelpful response: "Why are the voices telling you to do that?"

Helpful response: "I know the voices seem very real to you and you're scared not to do what they say, but they're really imaginary."

Helpful response: "I know you can't help hearing those voices, but they are not real and I hope you will try not to do what they tell you to."

Helpful response: "I understand that pointing has meaning to you, but I find it disturbing and I would like you to stop."

In this way you can serve as a mirror of reality. How successful you will be at it depends upon how you intervene as well as the severity of the existing thought disorder.

Frequently, disturbed people act on their bizarre ideas. A person who hears voices that give commands will attempt to carry out those commands. A person who believes the family is trying to poison him will refuse to eat and may run away. Sometimes, however, chronic mental patients engage in habitual inappropriate behavior for no apparent reason. One young woman walks the streets of her town, crying openly; she does not know why she does it. A young man insists that a certain chair in the house is his, that even when he is not home, no one may sit in it; he becomes aggressive if they do. An elderly lady rocks back and forth in a chair, seemingly unable to sit still. A middle-aged man giggles to himself and makes strange faces, even in church. Behaviors like these, while not dangerous, can cause the family great embarrassment.

Although the ill relative may not be able to stop them altogether, he can learn to confine odd behaviors to certain times or places. But the family must first decide if a particular behavior is really intolerable in a particular setting. Is the control of this behavior really a top priority? If so, they can request, in a simple and nonemotional way, that the disturbed member change his behavior, and can also make a statement about the consequences of future behavior:

> John, I know that it is hard to remember not to talk to yourself, but it is very disturbing in church. We have decided not to take you with us unless you are able to control it there.

> Janet, I know you want me to take you to the concert next week. I am willing to take you if you succeed in not crying in front of people who aren't in the family between now and then.

If a consistently applied strategy works, fine. If not, it is possible that the person cannot control the annoying behavior or that the reward is not a powerful enough motivator. Another explanation might be that the disturbing behavior itself carries some hidden reward—perhaps attention from family members. So do not give up after one failure. Needless to say, it is crucial to follow through on both the rewards and the punishments you have set up.

Ability to Work

Families frequently want to know, "Why can't my relative get [or hold] a job? Will he [or she] ever be able to work?" This same lack of motivation and disturbed thinking make getting and holding a job difficult. The disturbed person may have trouble remembering a set of instructions or keeping his mind on the task at hand. Having failed many times in the past, he may have a low tolerance for frustration. He is likely to give up easily if the task seems complicated, prolonged, or just boring.

Feeling stigmatized by their illness, these individuals may feel uncomfortable in the work place and may worry about not being as good as the next guy. These worries can consume so much energy that work actually suffers. Those who are withdrawn or have poor social skills may feel particularly handicapped on the job. In addition, people who become ill during their late teens or early adulthood may have missed the opportunity to develop a vocation or even good work habits. For them, the thought of a competitive job may be particularly frightening.

Yet many mentally ill people are able to work. Some need a sheltered setting or part-time work. Others will not be able to achieve at a level consistent with their intelligence or education. How is the family to know if their relative will be able to work? There is no way to know for sure, but certain factors do come into play. People who have worked prior to their illness are more likely to be able to work than those who did not. People whose thinking disturbances are fairly minor are better candidates than those whose thinking processes are more impaired. Those who can derive some enjoyment from people, activities, and accomplishments will do better than those who cannot.

You can help your ill relative to achieve maximal work potential in a number of ways. First, as always, expect progress to come in small steps, not great leaps. Second, seek assistance from the local vocational rehabilitation agency, which can evaluate your relative's skills, suggest appropriate placement, and sometimes even pay for job training. And third, contact the local mental hospital or mental health center for referral to programs specifically designed to provide job training for chronic mental patients.

There may be sheltered workshops in your community in which your relative can earn some money while gaining work skills and self-confidence. Some people graduate from these programs into regular outside jobs. Others remain indefinitely in the workshop setting, which provides social stimulation and a sense of purpose for the ill person and time off for caretaking relatives.

If your relative is able to spend most of his time outside hospitals, chances are he will be able to engage in at least some constructive activity. Be aggressive in your search for suitable programs, and be firm in your request that he at least give them a try.

Immaturity

Typically, chronic mental patients seem emotionally younger than their age. Many seem perpetually caught at the adolescent stage of development, outwardly clamoring for responsibility and independence while inwardly feeling vulnerable and afraid. One perceptive father says of his son:

> He'd talk about leaving . . . he said something about running away from home. I said to him, "If you want to go, you can go." And when it came right down to it, he couldn't leave. He realized in his own mind that he was incapable of making it alone. This also angers him because he wants to be free, he wants to be able to operate on his own, and he's frustrated because he can't do it. And of course he blames us for it, as if we were keeping him here, making him stay here.

Other people are more frankly dependent, asking family members to provide for their basic needs and to make all major decisions for them. Betty Lacey does Steve's shopping, laundry, and cleaning. She and Tom pay for his apartment out of his Social Security disability money, which they manage.

The majority of people with chronic mental illness may seem somewhat irresponsible and self-centered, apparently unaware of the needs of others and unable to tolerate for very long not getting what they want. One woman says of her mother:

> Through all those suicide attempts, I always came to the rescue, every time. Yet from the day I got engaged until my son was born, two and a half years later, I had almost no relationship with my mother. She didn't see my wedding gown until the day before the wedding. She never saw the apartment. Nothing. I was very angry and very hurt. Later, when she started having problems with her husband, she started coming over to the house occasionally.

When any family member is childish, demanding, and selfish, it is very difficult for other family members to continue caring for and about that person without resentment. When that family member is chronically mentally ill, the resentment is tempered by feelings of guilt. Although these feelings are perfectly normal and can never be completely resolved, being aware of the source of the person's self-centered immaturity can help to relieve them somewhat. Understanding this aspect of the person's behavior is particularly important because improvement in this area is usually very slow or nonexistent.

Incapacitating illness almost always causes the sufferer to become more self-centered. This is as natural in chronic mental illness as in physical illness and can also be seen in many elderly people. In fact, most of us can observe this tendency within ourselves when we are in the midst of even a temporary illness. We want to be relieved of the responsibility of caring for ourselves or others.

This feeling of helplessness is coupled with the sense of inadequacy and fear of failure, which accompany mental illness. Remember that your relative may have been ill during a time when his or her peers were "growing up" emotionally. Many important and valuable developmental experiences may have been missed.

The family that is able to develop expectations and responses that are consistent with their ill member's emotional age find they are more comfortable than the family that continues to expect the individual to "act his age." This latter family is likely to be continually frustrated and hurt. "He doesn't give a damn about us" is a common refrain. It may help to remember that he cares as much as he is able, considering how worried he is about himself.

Impulsiveness

Of serious concern to family members are the kinds of poor

judgment illustrated in the following three examples.

- Terry was in a car accident and suffered extensive brain damage when she was fifteen years old. Although she recovered many of her abilities, she became truant from school, sexually promiscuous, and an abuser of alcohol and drugs. She just does whatever she wants at the moment, with no thought of the longer-term consequences of her behavior.

- Adam, who suffers from mood swings, is a junior high school teacher. When he is elated, he ignores the clock and lectures on and on—continuing even after the last student has left the room. His lectures are filled with unseemly sexual references. He has depleted the family finances by paying a publisher to publish his "master work," which is incomprehensible.

- Bob develops strange and frightening ideas about God and the devil from time to time. During the most recent episode of agitation, he cut his arm with a razor "to see what color my blood really is."

Most forms of chronic mental illness impair the individual's ability to develop and implement long-term plans. Impulsive, self-defeating, or self-destructive behaviors are relatively common. Judgment is frequently impaired. Unfortunately, there is often little that families can do about this distressing and potentially dangerous group of symptoms. Demanding that the individual exhibit better judgment tends to be ineffective. Requests that a specific behavior be changed may have somewhat better success. Probably the best strategy is to try to arrange the circumstances so that the person's poor judgment does not have catastrophic consequences.

Terry's family, for example, has not been able to stop her

promiscuous behavior, but they have convinced her to use birth control. At least she will avoid the additional responsibility of an unwanted baby. While Terry does not see her drug-taking as a problem, her family does. They have not been able to get her to stop using drugs or to accept counseling, but they are careful not to keep medication or alcohol at home in any quantity, because they know she will take almost anything she finds. They also have learned to recognize the signs of drug overdose and have taken Terry to the hospital twice for treatment. They know they cannot prevent her from getting alcohol and drugs from her friends, and they are aware of the very real possibility that she could accidentally kill herself. However, at least they are doing what they can do to minimize the risk.

Adam and the principal at the school have developed an agreement whereby Adam must be evaluated by his psychiatrist when the principal sees signs of deteriorating performance. In effect, Adam will be allowed to teach only with the permission of his physician. If he breaks this agreement, his employment will be terminated. Although Adam is not pleased with the control this agreement takes from him and gives to his psychiatrist, he is aware that he has already given the school ample reason to fire him.

Since Bob lives alone in an apartment, it is difficult for his family to keep a close watch on him. However, his sister has made arrangements for a visiting nurse to see him three times a week. She and her other siblings call or stop by the other four days a week. They cannot be sure they will prevent a catastrophe, but they have been able to judge the severity of his condition with reasonable accuracy and have intervened effectively by getting him more intensive treatment from time to time.

Violence
While rarer than most people think, threats, abuse, and actual attack do occur with some individuals who suffer from chronic mental illness.

• Adam, the junior high school teacher, age forty-seven, has a history of severe mood swings. During periods of elation, he has numerous strange ideas, one of which is that his college girl friend has divorced her husband and is waiting somewhere for him. In the past, frightened that his wife would somehow prevent him from leaving, Adam has lost control when she has attempted to "talk some sense into him." On one occasion she suffered a broken and bloody nose. On another, she emerged with three cracked ribs.

One way that you can help minimize violent incidents is to become aware of signs that indicate your disturbed relative is losing control of aggressive feelings. Like the rest of us, mentally ill people are most likely to become aggressive when they feel cornered or attacked. Therefore, signs of increasing fear or discomfort, such as agitation, disorganization, suspiciousness, or withdrawal, may signal aggressive intent.

When such signs are present, it is unwise to crowd the disturbed individual, either physically or emotionally. Perhaps he needs some time alone. Under no circumstances should you physically impose yourself upon your relative, since this will increase his anxiety and reduce his self-control. Even attempting to comfort him with a hug may be a mistake at these times. A general principle in dealing with a highly agitated person is not to make any physical approach without his request. It is also useful to allow your disturbed relative an avenue of escape, so do not remain alone behind closed doors. Family members may be concerned that their relative might hurt an innocent stranger, but such a worry is usually unfounded. The individual rarely wants to hurt someone. If he can escape from the situation, he will probably do so and violence will be avoided.

Likewise, this is the wrong time to dispute your relative's irrational ideas. It is, however, a good time to acknowledge your relative's feelings and your willingness to try to understand what he is experiencing. Remember, though, *offer* to discuss his feelings; do not *insist* upon it. For example, Adam's wife might usefully say:

> I can see you really feel the need to look for your old girl friend, and you don't want me to try to stop you. I won't. Would it be helpful to talk more about your feelings with me or with your doctor?

While you will surely be frightened, it will help if you can remain calm. Frequently such individuals greatly fear their own loss of control. Your own fearful behavior may increase your relative's panic and the likelihood of violence. If you communicate that you expect your relative to remain in control, he is actually more able to do so.

A family will sometimes develop a strategy for reducing their relative's aggression that we definitely *do not* recommend. This involves giving in to the person's every demand, in the hopes of preventing a crisis. Recall, for example, that Betty Lacey, afraid of a confrontation between Tom and Steve, hid her bruises under long sleeves. Although early on Steve only shoved her when he was extremely agitated, his behavior gradually deteriorated to the point that he would slap or push her for failing to change a television station at his command. The result is often that families like the Laceys feel like prisoners in their own homes. Not only does this strategy necessitate great sacrifice on the part of the well family member, but we have no evidence that it works! What it does usually do is provoke the disturbed relative to escalate his demands and use threats of violence to enforce them.

Even if you follow all of the guidelines, there may be aggressive outbursts that you are unable to prevent. At such times you must take whatever steps are necessary to protect yourself and others from injury. This may mean leaving your agitated relative alone while you go for help, or it may mean locking him in a room. This may be highly embarrassing, but you must get

help from other relatives, neighbors, even the police if necessary.

Families often resist calling police or medical authorities out
of fear of permanently alienating their disturbed relative. They
loathe the thought of punishing him for something over which
he has no control. They do not want to admit that they are
unable to handle their own problems without help. However,
quick, effective control is therapeutically important as well as
necessary for the protection of others. First, the police may be
in a much better position to secure treatment for your relative
than you are. Second, you must communicate to your relative
that no matter how upset he may be, he will not be allowed
to hurt anyone. Failure to do this increases the likelihood of
further aggression. It is a mistake to tolerate moderately aggressive behavior (like a punch in the arm or a shove against the
wall) in the hopes that it will not get any worse. Such a strategy
almost guarantees that it *will* get worse, since it lowers the
person's motivation to exert self-control.

Mentally ill people are typically dismayed by their own aggressive behavior when they begin to recover. They are often
grateful to family members who have prevented them from
doing damage. Providing external constraints is a favor, not a
betrayal. Physical violence can be reduced by communicating
understanding and accepting feelings while at the same time
making it clear that aggression will not be tolerated.

Suicide

Delusional ideas, despair, and impulsivity all contribute to a
high risk of suicide. Since suicides among disturbed people may
occur without warning or apparent reason, it is impossible for
the family to prevent their disturbed relative's suicide by sheer
vigilance. However, although suicide attempts, like aggressive
outbursts, may occur without warning, they are sometimes
preceded by signals of distress. Families should respond to
these signs, particularly when they occur in people who have

made suicide attempts in the past. Among the indicators of possible suicide intent are

1. Feelings of personal worthlessness or concerns about having committed an unpardonable sin
2. Painfully hopeless attitude toward the future, particularly in those people who are *recovering* from an acute worsening of their condition
3. The presence of hallucinatory voices that instruct the person to hurt or kill himself
4. A sudden, inexplicable brightening of mood in a person who had been seriously, chronically depressed
5. Attempts to get one's affairs in order, including writing a will, patching up old disputes, or visiting an attorney
6. Discussion of concrete, specific suicidal plans

Paradoxically, suicide is less likely for individuals whose illness is marked by apathy and listlessness and more likely for those who continue to struggle toward personal and social goals. This is probably related to the disparity between the person's ambitions and accomplishments. Recognition of this disparity does not occur immediately but develops gradually after a series of acute episodes of illness. The individual becomes less and less able to pick up the pieces and begin again, less and less confident that he can finish what he starts.

If your relative does seem suicidal, you can help in two ways. First, recognize his distress. Do not ignore his communications. Emotional support is essential to the depressed person. Minimizing his problems and denying the validity of his feelings only increase his sense of alienation and loneliness. The following are examples of *nonhelpful* responses:

What are you worried about? With your intelligence you ought to be able to accomplish anything.

I'm sure everything will work out fine if you just cooperate with the doctor.

Look on the bright side. Things are bound to get better.

Stop moping around. There are people in a lot worse shape than you are.

Instead, you might say something like:

It's really depressing to think that you might not ever be able to finish college. I guess that sometimes you feel that it's just not worth the struggle anymore.

But more than that is necessary. You should get your relative to a mental health practitioner, who can evaluate the need for medication, counseling, or inpatient treatment. You need not, and should not, bear the responsibility for deciding what to do alone. Often you will be able to convince your relative to seek help just by communicating your genuine concern and wish to help. Sometimes, though, you may have to have your relative evaluated against his will. This is particularly likely in the case of individuals who are responding to hallucinations or who may feel that committing suicide is consistent with God's will. The police, a suicide prevention center, or possibly a mental health crisis unit can be most helpful under these circumstances.

Chronic mental illness is accompanied by a variety of problematic behaviors, ranging in severity from the merely embarrassing to the immediately life-threatening. Many of these behaviors are within the individual's control most of the time. You can be quite successful in modifying your disturbed relative's behaviors if you will follow these principles:

1. Develop a list of behaviors that you would like to help your relative change. Begin with the most dangerous or disturbing behaviors, and focus your attention and energy on them. Do not make the mistake of targeting trivial behaviors instead of serious ones. Do not, for example, spend time figuring out how to get your relative to take showers when he is terrorizing the household with aggressive threats. *Take first things first.*

2. Develop a consistent and clear approach to the behaviors in question. Ideally, all family members should agree on how to respond to the problematic behaviors. If rewards and punishments are involved, make sure your relative knows exactly what is expected of him and is aware of the consequences you have specified. Be clearer and more specific than you think you need be. Try to ensure that each task is within your relative's capability, particularly early on. Most importantly, *follow through.*

3. Do not waste energy arguing, threatening, or pleading. These strategies succeed only in raising the level of anxiety both you and your relative feel. When anxiety goes up, competence and self-control go down.

4. If a task is complicated, break it down into smaller units. Be aware of, and appreciative of, small, step-by-step improvements. If your goals are unrealistic and you fail to notice the positive changes your relative is making, everyone's motivation is likely to collapse. Keep yourself and your relative going by acknowledging small steps forward.

Do not become upset with yourself when you fail to follow these principles. Remember that you are bound to make mistakes. If you fall into an unproductive argument with your disturbed relative, ask him to change too many things at once, or make your requests in a way he cannot understand, it is no disaster. Usually you have lost nothing but a little time.

10

The Family's Involvement with Treatment

The previous two chapters reviewed some of the issues that arise in day-to-day living with your mentally ill relative. This chapter discusses some of the more general responsibilities that may be involved in your role as caretaker.

Medication

Most chronic mental illnesses require prolonged medication, and in many cases continuation of this medication is the crucial factor in the person's ability to remain in the community. The individual and caretaking family members should obtain a clear understanding of the type, purpose, and potential side effects of the medication. If the person has been hospitalized, it is likely that the appropriate type and dosage of medication will have been determined sometime before release. Someone who has not been in the hospital or was admitted only briefly may require a period of adjustment and may undergo some dosage changes while living at home.

Many different kinds of medications are used in the treatment of mental illness. These drugs, called psychotropics, include medications that are antipsychotic (sometimes called major tranquilizers), antidepressive (or mood elevators), minor tranquilizers, and medications to counter side effects produced by the other drugs. The table on page 141 lists some of these drugs by both their chemical (generic) and brand names. Antipsychotic drugs act to reduce disordered thinking, calm runaway feelings, and allow the individual to control his behavior. These medications generally enable the individual to function and to participate more constructively in other forms of treatment. The effect of minor tranquilizers is to control anxiety and tension. They have a widespread use and are common in treating transient periods of anxiety as well as more chronic conditions. The antidepression medications primarily treat depressive states that are not precipitated by environmental stress. Rather, they are effective with depression that seems to be related to internal biochemical changes. Some medications that are a combination of tranquilizer and antidepressant (for example, Triavil, Etrafon) are designed to help individuals whose symptoms include both anxiety and depression. Lithium carbonate is used specifically in the treatment of manic-depressive illness and at times in other illnesses that have a manic-depressive component. Finally, there are medications designed to alleviate side effects sometimes encountered in the use of the other drugs.

Side effects vary widely from individual to individual, from medication to medication, in severity and in duration. Some people never experience any side effects, while others encounter several. Some side effects that generally occur early in treatment (and primarily with the antipsychotic medications) are drowsiness, dryness of the mouth, faintness, palpitations, nasal stuffiness, and a drop in blood pressure. These effects usually disappear after a few weeks. More prolonged side effects include tremors, a feeling of restlessness (referred to as akathisia), and dystonia (rigidity of the face, head, and neck muscles). These symptoms are generally treated with other drugs aimed at the reduction of side effects. Some of the antipsychotic medications can produce a sensitivity to sunlight, which requires extra protection from sunburn. One side effect that has been linked to prolonged and heavy use of antipsychotic medication is tardive dyskinesia, involving involuntary peculiar tongue and mouth movements. It may be irreversible, and early warning signs may necessitate a change in medication.

One effect of medication that many patients and families notice (particularly when first prescribed) is a sort of zombie-like demeanor. The individual may respond to the sedating effects of the medication by feeling and looking drowsy and vacant. This effect generally decreases or disappears as the person adjusts to the medication or as the acute episode subsides and the medication dosage is reduced.

Some of the drugs, such as lithium carbonate or the monoamine oxidase (MAO) inhibitors, must be monitored particularly closely, and some diet restrictions are imposed. For example, people taking MAO inhibitors may not eat cheese and certain other foods, since serious side effects, such as severe headaches or coma, could result. With these drugs it is especially important to adhere strictly to the instructions given by the prescribing physician.

The variety of medications available allows a physician to try different medications with an individual who does not respond to one or who experiences uncomfortable side effects. Often dosages can be altered so that side effects are less troublesome. As with any medication, the risk of side effects must be weighed against the advantages of use. The psychiatric medications, in spite of the occasional unpleasant effects, enable many people to function and live in the community who otherwise could not do so.

Depending on the reliability of the ill family member, other family members may be at least in part responsible for monitoring medication to make sure that the individual is receiving it properly. However, there may be disagreement over whether or not the disturbed person should handle the medication. This dispute should be worked out openly within the family so that everyone is clear about how the medication will be dispensed. It is not helpful to agree to let your relative handle the medication and then surreptitiously check to see if the "promise" is being kept. A hands-off policy by the well family members may be very difficult and frightening to maintain. However, if this is the way that the ill member wishes to handle things, the others are only promoting needless conflict by insisting otherwise.

You can also keep in mind that if your relative wishes to discontinue his medication, he can do so easily, even if it is being given to him, by simply not swallowing it. It is quite natural to worry about the discontinuation of medication, especially when it may be vital to your relative's continued progress. Nevertheless, this is a situation that requires some restraint to avoid unnecessary tension. Similarly, some family members worry that their relative will abuse the medication or use it in suicidal gestures or attempts. This concern, too, should be voiced openly, and some agreement should be reached by all family members. If it is agreed that the individual is going to handle it, the family members should remember that there are many ways to commit suicide. If their relative is determined to try, overdosing on prescribed medication is not the only way of achieving such a goal. If your family decides that a well family member should help administer the medication, it is especially important to be familiar with the medication and to be careful to administer the proper dosages.

Irrespective of who assumes responsibility for medication, family members will also want to be alert for side effects and should feel free to consult the doctor about disturbing signs. This raises another difficult issue for families: how to distinguish between medication side effects and behavior that is under the individual's control. A typical example is tiredness. People on medication frequently complain of sleepiness or fatigue, and both families and professionals are often hard pressed to know if the excessive sleeping is due to medication, boredom, depression, or lack of motivation. This situation can be handled similarly to the problem of distinguishing "ill" from "normal" behavior discussed in Chapter 8. A trial-and-error method of testing whether a particular symptom is present under varying circumstances may help determine its origin. For instance, if the ill member lies around the house sleeping but is ready to participate in recreational activities at any time with no apparent fatigue, then it is unlikely that the sleeping is due to the medication. The family can give encouragement as well for their relative to overcome any fatigue that might be medication-related by keeping busy and adhering to a routine. If some symptoms do appear to be directly caused by the medication, the doctor should be consulted.

Because of potentially serious side effects of medication (especially the antipsychotics), some mental health professionals suggest "drug vacations," periods when the patient's medication should be discontinued. However, discontinuation of medication should be undertaken only in close consultation with your physician and under careful supervision of your relative. Overall, if your relative responds well to medication, it is advisable to stay on it.

Families often do not understand and are angered by their relatives' reluctance to continue taking their medication. A pattern may develop in which a person agrees to take medication for some period of time and then discontinues somewhat abruptly. This can happen repeatedly even when subsequent problems can be predicted. There are many reasons for this pattern, including uncomfortable side effects, overconfidence during remission, rebellion against "patienthood," and a resentment of the "boredom" of sanity. Many people find themselves more constricted and inhibited during remissions and feel that they are enjoying themselves more when they are free of the "toning-down" effects of medication. A person whose illness consists partly of feeling very elated and powerful may miss these feelings when they are treated with medication that is subduing. It is not clear whether the feelings of emptiness and boredom that many people report are due to the medication or whether these feelings simply emerge during remission. Regardless, an individual sometimes feels that the euphoria associated with his illness is more desirable than the empty feelings that arise when he is better. This is an extremely difficult issue that requires an acceptance by the ill person that some sacrifices are necessary in order to remain stable. Although the remission phase may feel somewhat empty, it also represents a marked increase in the individual's ability to control behavior and to function productively. The individual may have to live without the "excitement" of psychosis in order to achieve the self-esteem of sanity.

A final major reason for discontinuation of medication is that long-term medication reaffirms the chronic nature of the illness. Families may dislike the idea of long-term medication for this reason. Chronic mental illness requires chronic treatment, and the acceptance of this long-term treatment indicates a willingness to accept the chronicity.

Families' involvement with medication must also involve alertness to the signs of psychiatric deterioration. Families frequently recognize prepsychotic symptoms before professionals, since they have had many more opportunities to observe them. The Laceys, for instance, had become quite familiar with signs of oncoming illness.

> When two things happen, I know he's really sick again. One, he wants to cut his hair, and two, he says he doesn't need glasses. He's blind as a bat. When he wants his glasses back, I know he's better.

Families can also pick up signs that medication is no longer being taken or that it is not working in time to prevent further deterioration. Disturbed individuals can be taught to be more aware of their own prepsychotic patterns and thereby aid both their families and their therapists in helping them to maintain stability.

You can be extremely helpful to mental health professionals

by keeping a list of the medications that have been tried and your relative's response to each one. You may be able to suggest what medication could help during a crisis by recalling successful responses in the past. Not all professionals are receptive to the family's help, but some will appreciate tremendously this information.

Many families ask about the use of vitamins and diet to treat chronic mental illness. Some practitioners and researchers have postulated that massive doses of vitamins or dietary restrictions reduce psychiatric symptoms. There is no sound clinical proof to substantiate these ideas. Families should treat this type of treatment with extreme caution, particularly if it is to be used instead of standard psychiatric medication.

Shock Therapy

Electroconvulsive therapy (ECT) often conjures up horrible visions for family members and their ill relatives. They think of earlier times when "shock treatments" were associated with violent tempers, maybe even broken bones. In fact, the ECT of today is not a horrendous sight and is painless. Muscle relaxants and anesthesia are usually given prior to the administration of the treatment. Electrodes are attached on either side of the forehead and a shock is given. Generally only a slight tremor is observable. The patient is unconscious during the treatment and awakens within several minutes, though there may be some confusion for an hour or so afterward. Electroconvulsive therapy usually consists of two or three treatments per week for a few weeks. Some physicians give maintenance treatments once a week for a few more weeks. It can be done on an inpatient or outpatient basis.

One risk of ECT is memory loss. Most individuals regain their memory gradually and suffer no permanent loss, but there are some instances reported of long-term memory deficits. These difficulties appear to occur primarily among elderly people who undergo the treatment.

ECT is used considerably less frequently since the advent of antipsychotic drugs. At the current time, it is used primarily for acute depression when there is a risk of suicide or severe self-destructive behavior. For such a condition it has been shown to be a fast and effective treatment and can be a valuable adjunct to other types of therapy. There is, however, continued controversy over its use and effectiveness in treating schizophrenia.

If ECT is recommended by your relative's physician, you can certainly request another opinion. If you are absolutely opposed to such treatment, you can withhold your consent. You will certainly want to weigh all the alternatives and determine what may be most helpful in reducing your relative's symptoms.

Finances

Management of finances is another area in which families generally take some part. In some instances their role is legally defined and in others it is outlined by mutual agreement. For instance, Dan was appointed "payee" by the Social Security Administration and is responsible for handling Karen's disability benefits. This means that he must divide the monthly payments among treatment costs, Karen's current personal expenses, and her future needs. Dan must keep good records of all transactions to avoid confusion or dispute with Karen or with the government.

Even a family member who is not legally responsible for finances may reach an agreement with his relative to handle some aspects of financial management. Both parties should be clear about who will be responsible for what, and if at all possible, the ultimate goal should be for the ill person to manage his own budget. As we have stressed before, any independent functioning that is possible should be encouraged. As in other areas, money management can be approached gradually, allowing the person to make decisions first about small personal expenses and later about more substantive expenses.

Psychosocial Treatment

Families are also involved with other forms of treatment, such as day hospital, sheltered workshop, and vocational training, which will be described in more detail in Chapter 11. Families wonder how much they should push their relatives to be involved in these activities. One mother reported that she transported her daughter to a sheltered workshop program daily even though this meant giving up her job. She became uncertain that this was worthwhile when her daughter began to frequently oversleep or think up excuses not to attend.

> I'd sit around here waiting until noontime and then [she'd] say, "Well, I'm not going today . . ." I did that for weeks and weeks, and finally I said, "Either you make the commitment to go and participate in the program, or I'm going to do my own thing."

Families must reach a satisfactory resolution of the conflict between personal sacrifice for and support of their ill relatives. Remember that no matter how much investment and work you put in, the chief responsibility for the maintenance of treatment lies with the ill person. He must be the one who *chooses* to continue treatment, since cooperation itself will determine in large part its success. The family can be ready to provide support, but they cannot in the long run provide the motivation.

Another treatment area in which families become involved is family therapy. Families are frequently asked by mental health professionals to enter some form of treatment themselves, either with or without their relative. This treatment may be time-consuming, but family members frequently find that contact with treatment personnel is helpful both to their relative and to themselves.

Finally, of considerable importance in providing for your relative is helping him develop and maintain his own emotional supports. Just as the ill member needs social contacts outside of the family, so the family needs time off from caretaking duties. Both professional treatment facilities and peers can meet these needs. Often the family finds that their relative functions best when bolstered not only by the support of family but also by an individual therapist, a therapy group, or an organization like Alcoholics Anonymous. A chronically ill person may need to "touch base" with at least one of these on a semi-regular basis for reassurance and constancy.

Peers can provide gratification and reward. If your relative does not already have a set of friends, peer relationships can be formed in various treatment facilities, church groups, community college courses, bowling leagues, and job settings, to name a few.

Another support, available in some communities, is to have a volunteer companion come and visit your ill relative. Such people are frequently more successful than family members or professionals at encouraging the person to try new experiences. Volunteer programs of this kind may be organized by colleges, churches, and other organizations and can usually be located through the local mental health center or mental health association.

A family may sometimes hold the belief that associating with other disturbed persons can only make their relative worse. They feel that he would be better off avoiding friends made in the hospital and staying away from programs for ex-patients. This is definitely not true. Such settings provide a safe environment in which to practice social skills. The person is assured that he will not be severely criticized for social blunders and is able to feel at ease with others who are "in the same boat." Many people can and do go beyond this social system in time; others who are more disturbed may find that they are comfortable only in a social situation with few pressures. Even in these cases the individual's horizons are substantially wider than those of a person who remains isolated at home. If family members can help provide encouragement and opportunities for their relative to establish peer relationships, they will probably find that this, of all the care provided, will have the most beneficial and rewarding effect.

Psychiatric Medications

Antipsychotic Drugs	*(Generic Name)*	*Uses*
Haldol	(Haloperidol)	Illnesses in which
Inapsine	(Droperidol)	disturbed thinking
Loxitane	(Loxapine)	is a major symptom.
Mellaril	(Thioridazine)	These include
Moban	(Molindone)	schizophrenia and
Navane	(Thiothixene)	senile dementia,
Proketazine	(Carphenazine)	among others.
Prolixin	(Fluphenazine)	Also effective for
Quide	(Piperacetazine)	short-term control
Serentil	(Mesoridazine)	of agitated,
Sparine	(Promazine)	aggressive behavior.
Stelazine	(Trifluoperazine)	
Taractan	(Chlorprothixene)	
Thorazine	(Chlorpromazine)	
Tindal	(Acetophenazine)	
Trilafon	(Perphenazine)	
Vesprin	(Triflupromazine)	
Lithium Carbonate		Primarily for manic-depressive illness.

Minor Tranquilizers

Atarax	(Hydroxyzine hydrochloride)	To control anxiety.
Equanil	(Meprobamate)	
Librium	(Chlordiazepoxide hydrochloride)	
Serax	(Oxazepam)	
Tranxene	(Chlorazepate dipotassium)	
Valium	(Diazepam)	

*Antidepressive
Drugs*

Elavil	(Amitriptyline)	To reduce depression.
Imavate	(Imipramine Hydrochloride)	
Norpramin	(Desipramine hydrochloride)	
Sinequan	(Doxepin hydrochloride)	
Tofranil	(Imipramine hydrochloride)	
Vivactil	(Protriptylene hydrochloride)	
Triavil and Etrafon	(Perphenazine and Amitriptyline)	When both disturbed thinking and depression are apparent.

MAO Inhibitors

Eutonyl	(Pargyline hydrochloride)	To reduce depression.
Marplan	(Isocarboxazid)	
Nardil	(Phenelzine sulfate)	
Parnate	(Tranylcypromine sulfate)	

Side-Effect Drugs

Akineton	(Biperiden hydrochloride)	To alleviate restlessness and/or muscle rigidity.
Artane	(Trihexyphenidyl hydrochloride)	
Benadryl	(Diphenhydramine hydrochloride)	
Cogentin	(Benztropine mesylate)	

11

Negotiating the
Mental Health Maze

Mental health professionals are part of a vast and confusing bureaucracy that can appear formidable to families already overwhelmed and overburdened. This chapter provides an overview of the mental health maze and some suggestions for seeking help.

Community Mental Health Center
Let us suppose that your relative has become acutely ill and you have decided to seek help. How should you proceed? Community mental health centers are located throughout the country,. each one serving a particular geographic area (called a "catchment" area). The services offered by these centers vary widely but usually include a range of outpatient, diagnostic, and referral services as well as aftercare for posthospitalized patients. Others may also provide small inpatient units, emergency services, housing programs, vocational counseling, educational services, and partial hospitalization. These centers receive funds from federal, state, and local governments as well as from the private sector. The range of services will probably

depend on their funds. Many centers can help families find adequate hospitalization, give referrals to day programs, provide medication maintenance, and offer various forms of outpatient therapy (individual, group, family). Generally the telephone operator, your family physician, the local hospital or mental health association should know the name and location of the mental health center that serves you. In an emergency, you may also call the police or local crisis service, which will direct you to the proper treatment facility.

Hospitals

If your relative needs hospitalization, you will discover that there is a considerable range of hospitals with mental health facilities. Some general medical hospitals have small psychiatric units used primarily for short-term hospitalization and crisis intervention. Emergency rooms within general hospitals may offer crisis outpatient service and referrals for admission. Some community mental health centers offer inpatient treatment, primarily on an emergency or short-term basis. There are numerous private psychiatric hospitals that usually accept patients on a longer basis, but still do not generally provide lengthy care of several months or more. Generally these are affordable for only as long as insurance covers the bill. State or federally funded hospitals provide longer care at lower cost. Some private and state facilities provide numerous specialized services in addition to general psychiatric care. These may include alcohol- and drug-abuse rehabilitation programs, adolescent units, and geriatric care.

Hospitals generally provide several types of treatment, including medication, psychotherapy, vocational, occupational, and recreational therapy. Whether some or all of these treatments are provided will depend on the nature of each individual's problems and what the treatment staff feels will be most helpful.

You may be concerned about the restrictiveness of the hospital. However, this is designed to protect individuals who may be agitated, confused, or destructive. Hospitals allow for the resumption of greater freedom as soon as the individual exhibits self-control.

Commitment Procedures

When hospitalization is required, whether commitment is to be voluntary or involuntary becomes an issue. There is considerable controversy about the commitment laws and a diversity in procedures. The specific laws for commitment are state-regulated and therefore differ considerably from state to state. Generally, when a person *wishes* to receive inpatient treatment and is judged to *need* such treatment, admission is on a voluntary basis. Such an individual is free to leave at any point and participates in treatment planning. Involuntary commitment concerns those who are unwilling to receive inpatient treatment but who are judged in need of it. Who does the judging and what defines need are major focuses of a controversy that we will discuss at greater length in the next chapter.

Regardless, involuntary commitment is a painful experience for the entire family. If your relative has been involuntarily committed, he may blame not only the mental health and legal systems, but also the family member who was the petitioner or who gave testimony. Even if he later realizes that there was a need for involuntary treatment and feels he benefited from it, he may resent the process. If you must resort to involuntary commitment, be prepared for this resentment and for your own disheartenment at having to proceed in this manner.

One couple who petitioned for a commitment hearing for their daughter felt that a certain degree of familial trust and unity had been lost forever. Their daughter had made a serious suicide attempt, and the family felt that they could not stand by and watch her succeed in a second attempt. After some time in the hospital, even the daughter felt relieved that she had not succeeded and that she was receiving treatment. Nevertheless, she resented having been "put on trial" and placed in a hospital against her will. Although the family knew that their daughter needed treatment, they felt tremendously sad in testifying about her illness and publicly airing her thoughts and behavior. Everyone in this family eventually agreed that hospitalization was the only way for the daughter to receive the treatment that eventually helped her to decide against suicide. However, the action necessary to obtain this treatment took its toll in energy, finances, dignity, and family unity.

The legal system may enhance the family's guilt and regret by pointing accusingly at the family in its attempt to "free" the individual. For a family already beleaguered by the stress of caring for their relative, involuntary commitment procedures can be devastating. Nevertheless, families may need to seek this commitment in order to protect themselves and their ill relatives from harm. If your relative has become grossly confused, agitated, assaultive, or self-destructive, involuntary commitment may be the only protection you can provide.

We would like to say more specifically what behaviors might lead you to seek involuntary commitment. Unfortunately, laws are not uniform across the country, and even in one state they can be subject to varying interpretations. In some states only an actual act of violence will do. Threats of intended harm may not be sufficient no matter how often they are made or how perilous they sound. In some areas inadequate care of oneself that could lead to a serious health problem may be grounds for commitment, while elsewhere a specific suicidal act is the necessary prerequisite.

An example of this variability in interpretation can be illustrated by the following: An individual walks out of his house with no clothes on in the dead of winter. His family, seeking an involuntary commitment, testifies that he had been quite delusional for some time and felt that nudity was essential to cleanse himself from evil insects that had invaded his body. A judge could interpret this act as a symptom of mental illness, an inappropriate and bizarre behavior that, if continued, could lead to overexposure, a serious threat to his welfare. Another judge might view the behavior as inappropriate but feel that it was only an instance of poor judgment or an impulsive spree. This judge might not view such an act as sufficient evidence of serious danger.

If you believe your relative needs involuntary commitment, seek further advice from your local mental health center and from a lawyer. They can inform you about the laws in your area and your chances of obtaining the commitment. Keep in mind, too, that their advice is not a guarantee and that even a situation that appears appropriate for involuntary commitment may be dismissed at the hearing. In addition to specific advice, you can also receive emotional support from sympathetic professionals and other families who have been through this experience.

One final note about commitments: There are emergency commitment procedures designed to hospitalize a person involuntarily for a very short period of time (usually a few days) for evaluation and treatment planning. If you have reason to believe that you might need to use this procedure at some time, it would be good to prepare for it in advance. Find out from your local mental health center what the procedure entails in your area. Can the police be called to transport your relative if necessary, or must a crime have been committed? Is there a mobile crisis unit available? Where must your relative be taken for evaluation? What family members are available and willing to help you if the need arises? When a crisis occurs, advance preparation can minimize feelings of panic and helplessness. Generally the person must be of immediate danger either to himself or to others in order to be eligible.

Outpatient Services

Once your relative has left the hospital, you will want to explore options for outpatient treatment. Many communities have partial hospitalization programs. Day hospitals generally provide a five-day-per-week program, which can serve as a transition from or alternative to full-time hospitalization. An inpatient stay may be avoided if a person is provided with the additional support and structure of a day program, which may include psychotherapy, medication supervision, occupational and recreational therapy, and vocational training. Day hospitals can serve not only as a treatment facility for the individual but also as a respite for the family. Night hospitals, less common but available in some areas, generally serve those who are employed in the community in the daytime but require some support at night. They usually offer therapy services and sometimes beds.

Since chronic mental illness is often accompanied by vocational impairment, training or retraining may be necessary. Sheltered workshop programs provide supervised employment for those who find regular full-time employment too stressful. These workshops provide factorylike work for which clients are paid hourly or by the amount produced. They serve as a good transition for a chronically ill person who may not have held a job in some time and who needs an opportunity to practice work skills. Some workshops limit the duration of the client's stay in the program, while others allow long-term employment.

Other vocational training programs may not be specifically directed to the mentally handicapped but are intended for anyone who has experienced a gap in his education or training for employment. The local vocational rehabilitation bureau can offer suggestions, programs, and sometimes funding for those who have been disabled and need further career development. The bureau can be located through the telephone book, local community mental health center or mental health association.

Private practitioners abound in the field of mental health. Many disciplines provide private psychotherapy, including psychiatry, psychology, social work, and marriage counseling, among others. Fees and type of therapy vary widely. Deciding whether a private therapist would be beneficial and selecting the appropriate therapist are difficult for many families. *You Are Not Alone: Understanding and Dealing with Mental Illness,* by Clara Park and Leon Shapiro (Little, Brown, 1976), discusses the various options at length. You should remember that you and your relative are *consumers* and that you have a right to appropriate and satisfactory service. You may find that a particular practitioner is not helpful and that you may need to try more than one until you feel comfortable with someone. Beware, however, that too much "shopping around" may indicate that you are having some trouble facing your difficulties or trusting someone to help you with them.

Finally, there are many professional and lay groups that can provide help and support. Alcoholics Anonymous and Alanon are examples of therapeutic groups that can be of enormous value to the alcoholic and his family. Recovery, Inc., a group of former patients who provide support and comfort to each other, has chapters nationwide and may hold meetings in your town.

Some communities offer case management services, in which an informed staff member who is aware of all the resources available refers each patient to the appropriate service. The case manager is also responsible for ensuring receipt of those services. The Visiting Nurses Association, available in many communities, will send a nurse to your home to give medication and supportive counseling. Support groups and organizations are listed on page 152.

Financial Help

Families discover very quickly that chronic mental illness is costly not only emotionally but also financially. Bills for therapy, hospitalization, and medicine can exhaust a family's funds, leaving them nothing for "luxury" items or even emergencies. One family, after spending $25,000 on treatment for their son, felt guilty about hospitalizing him in a state institution: "For years you had the stigma attached to those fences, those gates, those buildings . . . Confinement for the rest of your life was the specter we had . . . The state hospital was the last stop." They wondered whether the care they could have secured for their son if they had had more money would have helped him progress further.

You need not struggle alone with the costs of caring for your relative. Various government and private organizations may help with part of the financial burden. Medical insurance can help substantially, although coverage varies widely. It may pay for both inpatient and outpatient treatment for various periods of time and within certain cost limits. If further hospitalization is required beyond the coverage of the insurance, state hospitals can provide treatment according to the family's ability to pay. Community mental health facilities and many private agencies operate on a sliding-fee scale and will adjust bills according to the client's income. You should discuss the fee prior to receipt of service.

There are several federally funded programs that can ease financial strain as well. Your relative may qualify for Social Security disability, which is intended for those who have been employed at some time but have become disabled by illness and are no longer able to maintain gainful employment. Application may take time, but the benefits are often substantial. The Veterans Administration also provides funds for those who are disabled, as does the Supplemental Security Income program. Local public-assistance offices can be helpful in providing information about federal or state funds for which your relative may be eligible and how to go about obtaining them.

Volunteer organizations can help with finances somewhat more indirectly. They may offer food, transportation, or social events at reduced cost. These organizations may be church-sponsored, but they are generally nonsectarian in providing service.

Although some funds are available, money is increasingly becoming more difficult to obtain. The government's rules concerning elibility and length of support are frequently difficult to discover and then to comprehend. Further, what is therapeutic for an individual may interfere with receipt of funds. For instance, clients in a sheltered workshop program cannot earn too much money or they may lose their monthly public-assistance allotment. A similar dilemma occurred when the Laceys tried to save some money for Steve:

> I paid his rent, I paid his gas and electric, and then I saved the rest of it for the following month. There was about eighty dollars left over. I didn't stop the food stamps, but I didn't buy any. If you don't buy food stamps, they cut you off. So even if you're honest about something, it doesn't pay.

There is no question that the care of a chronically ill relative, either in the home or away from it, is exorbitantly costly and can quickly drain a family's financial resources. However, you should try to ease this financial strain by exerting considerable effort locating and applying for financial assistance.

Available Resources

Inpatient

Private hospital
General hospital with psychiatric unit
State hospital
Veterans Administration hospital
Community mental health center, emergency or crisis unit

Outpatient

Partial hospitalization (day or night hospital)
Private practitioners
Community mental health center
Veterans Administration outpatient center

Professional Organizations

American Medical Association Council on Mental Health
National Institute of Mental Health
National Association of Private Psychiatric Hospitals
American Psychiatric Association
Bureau of Vocational Rehabilitation
National Association of Social Workers
American Psychological Association
National Association for Mental Health

Helpful Groups

National Association for the Mentally Ill
Alcoholics Anonymous (and Alanon)
Mental Patients' Liberation Front
Mental Patients' Liberation Project
Recovery, Inc.
Schizophrenics Anonymous

Financial Assistance

Social Security Disability
Supplemental Security Income
Public Assistance

152

12

Patient Rights and Family Needs

The mental health system in this country has grown to include not only a complex array of services and agencies, but also the legal system. A complicated relationship now exists among the consumers of mental health services, including patients on the one hand and families on the other, the providers of these services, and the law that is designed to ensure satisfactory service delivery. In this chapter we discuss the issues and conflicts that arise when the rights of the individual and the needs of the family are pitted against each other.

Advocacy
   Mental health laws primarily protect the individual's civil rights as guaranteed by the Constitution. Advocacy programs, established to safeguard these rights, have sprung up throughout the country. Advocates attempt to protect the legal interests of their clients without assessing the rationality of these interests. They are involved in a wide range of issues, including commitment, the right to refuse treatment, improvement in and availability of community services, and elimination of dis-

criminatory practices against the mentally ill. At times you may perceive these legal advocates as pursuing avenues that are countertherapeutic for your relative or antagonistic to your own needs. However, they are working to ensure that your relative is protected from abuse.

The Right to Refuse Treatment

The right to liberty and free choice constitutes one of our most basic civil rights. We would probably all agree that a person has the right to choose his own physician and to decide among various treatment options if he becomes ill. Yet exercising this right is complicated in the case of mental illness because the person's capacity to reason and to make informed decisions may be seriously diminished. Therefore, the right to refuse treatment is highly controversial and represents one of the most difficult issues families must confront. They may be unable to hospitalize their relative when they feel it necessary, or they may find that just as things are going smoothly, their relative refuses necessary medication.

One family made many attempts to hospitalize their schizophrenic daughter, who spent hours in her room alone listening to voices, apparently absorbed in a fantasy world. She had stopped going out of the house at all and was no longer attending to her personal appearance or hygiene. Although the family knew that she required treatment, she refused any treatment on a voluntary basis. The laws in that state required that individuals be of harm to themselves or others in order for involuntary commitment to be imposed. Since this young woman had never made an assaultive attempt and was not specifically self-destructive, she was not "commitable." Her parents felt that their hands were tied. Their daughter needed treatment, but they could not secure it as long as she remained unwilling. They continued to provide maintenance care for her without the aid of professional treatment and without the supports that the system can provide.

This family viewed commitment as necessary to secure

needed treatment for their daughter. Legal advocates would insist, however, that it must also be seen in the context of depriving the individual of the right to liberty. Given this view, the family will have to persevere in locating help and exploring all avenues for obtaining treatment. This may involve multiple contacts with mental health facilities, referral agencies, and perhaps a lawyer who may be able to provide additional information and help with the mental health laws in the area.

An additional, although painful, option if a mentally ill relative is breaking the law is for the family to press criminal charges. One mother who lived alone with her seventeen-year-old son expressed desperation after several years of coping with her son's frequent drug abuse. When he was "high" he would be verbally abusive and disorderly. He usually apologized after each episode and appeared to be genuinely sorry for his behavior. Nevertheless, he continued to abuse drugs and refuse treatment. Because he was not considered an immediate threat to himself or others, he could not be admitted involuntarily to the local state mental hospital. His mother was at her wit's end, feeling unable to tolerate any future episodes but unable to secure treatment for her son. Eventually she decided to contact the police and institute criminal proceedings with the hope that somehow her son's problem would be recognized and treatment begun.

Once an individual enters the justice system, he can be transferred into the mental health system. Sometimes criminal charges are later dropped on the condition that the individual receive mental health treatment. We should caution, however, that this may not happen and your relative may remain confined in a penal rather than mental institution. If the behavior is uncontrollable and your relative is unwilling to accept hospitalization or deemed inappropriate for it, this may be the only recourse for removing him from your home. Families should be convinced that this is their only option, as they will be heavily criticized by many for such a course of action.

Confidentiality

Mental health professionals often find themselves in a dilemma regarding the patient's right to privacy versus the family's need to know and to help. Suppose, for example, that a patient who leaves the hospital against the treatment team's advice has told his therapist, but not his family, where he is going. Knowing full well that the family would be willing and able to retrieve the patient, the therapist is obliged not to tell them what he has been told in confidence.

Yet families have a strong need to understand what their relative's illness is and how to cope with it. They are asking not for a breach of confidentiality but simply for concrete advice. As one parent said:

> We need guidance and direction. We need a pat on the head or a kick in the pants once in a while . . . Just as the patient is suffering, we, too, are suffering, and we're suffering because of our inadequacies—where to go, what to do, or how to do it.

Most families want to be helpful and need to stress that they deserve the information and know-how to succeed in this endeavor.

You can also learn to be more assertive in communicating your observations of your relative. For instance, you may have had an opportunity to observe the impact of several different medications and might be able to proffer an opinion about the most helpful one. This can be highly valuable information to the treatment staff and represents a definitive way in which you can provide input.

You can also share your feelings and observations about your relative's areas of stress and past failures or successes at home, on the job, or at school. Your input can contribute to the guidance given to your relative.

Some professionals will view the family's active involvement defensively, particularly if they believe that the family is the source of the person's problems. With this attitude you may face an uphill battle to have your concerns and suggestions regarded with respect. Nevertheless, you should stand firm in your demand to express opinions and ask questions. You also retain the right to seek a second opinion. Do not allow yourself to be intimidated.

Living Arrangements

The last several years have witnessed a general reduction in the number of individuals in mental institutions and an increase in their return to the community. This trend has arisen for several reasons. First, the advent of psychiatric medications has produced a marked decrease in disabling symptoms. Second, individuals are entitled to live in the least restrictive environment possible. Third, it is generally believed that living within a community will better aid the individual's recovery. Fourth, it is presumed that community care is less costly. Unfortunately, the effect of deinstitutionalization has been to place everyone in an untenable position, since the anticipated array of alternative community services has not materialized.

Many hospitals are required by law to release patients as soon as they can function in any way outside the inpatient setting. Few suitable living arrangements in the community exist for the chronically mentally ill. There are far too few boarding homes, halfway houses, group homes, or even decent inexpensive rooms and apartments.

Since frequently the most protective environment outside the hospital is the patient's home, many practitioners look to the family as the most logical and convenient setting for these individuals. Sometimes the push from the legal system to release the patient makes professionals, in turn, push the patient onto the family, which perhaps is not ready or is reluctant to accept the relative back into the home.

One young man who was no longer actively suicidal was judged ready for release by the hospital. The family, however, felt uncomfortable about having him at home, because both parents worked and there would be no supervision for him at home during the day. They also felt emotionally burdened by his chronic depression. The mother commented:

> I think the major factor is not feeling safe leaving [him] alone . . . because if I can't go to work and keep my job, then we're in great trouble. That's the one thing . . . It would be very hard to be around [him] constantly . . .

A family that wishes to give up even a part of the responsibility for their relative may face condemnation from professionals. They may be viewed as weak, uncaring, or cruel. The needs of the family may be viewed as secondary to those of the ill relative, and their wish to obtain some relief may be ignored.

Nevertheless, many families do decide that their only option is to have their relative live away from home. Many situations can lead to this conclusion—the fear of physical violence, for example. If your relative is aggressive and threatening when acutely ill, you may fear even the remotest possibility of a relapse. One family whose son had attacked his brother several times definitely feared for their safety if he returned home after the current hospitalization. Although they were uncertain about where he would be able to live if they did not allow him home, they felt that their physical well-being was in jeopardy otherwise:

> We are directed by fear . . . It's a hell of a thing to put your own child out of the house without knowing where he's going to go, but I can't see that we have any alternatives.

Even if your relative is not violent, he may behave in ways with which you feel unable to live. These might include frequent temper tantrums, extremely poor hygiene, irregular hours, or refusal to stay on medication.

Or you may simply no longer have the physical and emotional energy to care for your chronically ill relative. Some family members have secretly wished that their relative would die so that the misery for both the patient and the family might be over. One mother whose daughter had disappeared suddenly and had not contacted her family remarked:

> I woke up Friday morning, and I thought Friday was going to be the day I was going to hear something . . . about a body, and I felt relief. As hard as it's going to be . . . it will be done. I will know where she is, I will not have to worry. . . . I will not have the constant nagging at the back of my mind . . . that you're not doing enough and when you are, you're thinking, "I really don't want to do this." . . . And that's why, I think maybe, Friday I was thinking, "Please God, let it be done. Let her be out of the misery, let me be out of the misery."

While this particular wish may seem cruel, it is quite natural and is probably an unspoken thought of many overburdened, tired, and worried family members. They may see their relative's situation as tragic or hopeless and view death as one way of putting an end to everyone's suffering.

Family members often feel relieved when their relative is hospitalized and they no longer have to cope with him. After one particularly trying time with their son, Steve, and his subsequent hospitalization, Tom Lacey commented:

> You know, after all those years in the hospital, I thought, "Does he really have to go?" It's a good thing.

> BETTY: It would have been worse; I could not keep him at home. I could not live knowing that he was living in the apartment like he was. He was so paranoid . . . The doctor thought he might even throw himself out the window, trying to escape from whoever it was. . . . He was a very scared person.

After witnessing Steve's agitation, the Laceys, understandably, viewed the hospital as the safest place for him to be.

Family members may also notice that life progresses in a much more relaxed, tension-free manner when their relative is in the hospital. They feel free to socialize with friends or just go out by themselves for an evening. They are not worrying constantly about how their relative is feeling or behaving.

Having noticed that life seems easier when their relative is not at home and having seen that in spite of all their efforts their relative experiences recurrent acute episodes, the family may reach the decision to no longer have their relative live with them. The Laceys arrived at this conclusion after numerous hospitalizations and subsequent attempts to keep Steve at home. Their decision, however necessary, was a painful one.

> Don't you think it hurts that our house is paid for and we got a room where our son could live and he can't even live with us? We have a place for him and there's no way in the world . . . I couldn't live with him now in the same place. . . . Hey, we're still father and son and there's a lot of love there.

Finally, both the family and mental health practitioner may feel that living at home is therapeutically unsuitable for the ill individual. A family may find that their daughter functions better when she is forced to be responsible for herself. The separation from her parents may "push" her to be more independent. She may learn to plan and cook her own meals, do her own shopping, pay her own bills—activities that she might not be required to do if she were living at home. In this case, the family's decision to have her live independently not only makes life less stressful for them, but also can increase her self-esteem and desire to maintain herself in the community.

Whatever the reasons for reaching this decision, it is important for you to try not to feel guilty about it. If family life is overly stressful with your relative at home, then the stress is not good for anyone. And, as we illustrated earlier, your relative may be forced to rely on heretofore unfound strengths and abilities. If you wish to have your relative live apart from you, frequent visits, phone calls, and letters can still provide much-needed support. Continued contact can give your relative the confidence and courage necessary to make a satisfactory adjustment. One young woman, after years of living with her parents, finally moved into her own apartment about three miles from her parents' home. They arranged for daily phone calls, twice-weekly visits for dinner, and occasional weekends together. With this frequent contact and support, she was able to manage in her own apartment. Gradually the visits became less frequent as she developed a greater sense of self-confidence and formed her own circle of friends.

Yet another option is to spell out clearly to your relative the circumstances under which he may live at home. You may feel better able to cope if your relative is out of the house for several hours a day. A requirement for living at home might then be part-time employment or involvement in a day hospital program. In this way you can endure the hardships by knowing that each day there will be some relief. Regardless of the stress it places upon them, some families may feel that there are just no alternatives or that they do not wish to have their relative live anywhere else.

Finally, you must make clear to professionals your desires and plans for future living arrangements for your relative. If you have concluded that it is not feasible for him to remain at home, you must not feel forced into making an alternate decision.

Family Treatment

Many families feel that any treatment they receive is strictly to benefit their ill relatives and not them. One woman felt "that it was all looked at as though this [family therapy] were to benefit them in understanding [the patient]. It was not to help us particularly." Many professionals do in fact initiate family therapy for the purpose of modifying the family's style of interacting in order to help the identified patient. The focus of the therapy is the family's impact on the patient's illness and behavior. The perspective of traditional family therapy is that the family is the source of the individual difficulty and that the individual's problem is a symptom of the disturbance in the family. This perspective leads to a type of treatment that aims to uncover the family pathology and treat the illness by altering disturbed family patterns.

A type of therapy that you may find more helpful and comforting is supportive family counseling. This approach is based on the perspective that there is a real illness in the disturbed relative, and that the family is coping with a trying and disruptive situation. According to this view, at least some of the family's apparent dysfunction is a result, not a cause, of their relative's illness. The goal of supportive family counseling is support for the well family members and reduction in stress for the benefit of well and ill members alike. From this type of counseling you can receive emotional support as well as concrete suggestions for decreasing tension and chaos at home. You can also be referred for individual therapy if it is needed. You have a right to receive this kind of supportive help that will reduce guilt and enhance coping skills. You may want to seek out this type of professional support in order to have your own needs met.

Consumerism

Finally, you have the right as a consumer of services to make an evaluation of the help you and your relative receive. You do not have to assume that whatever help you are given is all that is necessary and that you cannot ask for more. Decide whether you feel free to ask questions and whether your questions are being answered in a straightforward manner. You have a right to challenge, to assert your opinions, and to have information.

It is important that there be some congruence in the expectations for service between the giver and the recipient. You should make a point of stating your expectations clearly and requesting the professional do the same. If the gap is too wide, you may need to seek alternative help. In this regard, just as your ill relative has an opportunity to seek an advocate, you may also wish to have advocacy support. In this age of patient rights, family advocates may be somewhat more difficult to find, but they are available. They may be found within the mental health system, that is, a professional who is particularly supportive and sympathetic to your situation. Family groups also can provide suggestions and backing. If necessary, you may wish to consult a lawyer who is knowledgeable in the mental health field either to educate you about your rights or to provide legal support if rights are being neglected or abused.

In discussing families' consumerism, we have perhaps not sufficiently emphasized that you will too often encounter stumbling blocks, such as the nonsupportive legal system, critical professionals, and confusing government agencies. Government regulations can make obtaining information and assistance quite problematic. Many families can cite numerous examples of nonsupportive or critical advice given to them by professionals. Families often feel that they are viewed derogatorily and given little assistance by mental health practitioners: "There was this feeling of superiority on their part"; "I felt like we were really on trial." Since you may encounter this judgmental and nonhelpful attitude, you should make an effort to remain with those practitioners you find to be supportive and informative. They do exist and will be easier to find if you know what you want and seek them out with an open and cooperative attitude.

IV

SPECIAL PROBLEMS

13

Spouses and Parents

Spouses

When two people marry, they must learn to live with each other, develop shared goals, and build up realistic expectations of each other. This process takes time and often creates conflicts during its course. Nevertheless, it does take place and creates a feeling of union between two people. When something happens that makes it difficult or impossible for one of the spouses to fill his or her role, the effects can be emotionally and physically disruptive to the other spouse. Such is the case when a person finds himself married to a chronically mentally ill person.

There are many ways in which chronic mental illness can seriously disrupt the relationship between you and your spouse. The overall consequence is to make you feel as if you were no longer married to the person you had originally known. The changes forced on both you and your spouse by chronic mental illness bring into question the very notion of marriage.

Spouses of the chronically mentally ill frequently sense an emotional loss. There is less or no time for talking about each other's day, thoughts, and feelings. Previously shared daily events are superseded by the practical necessities of care. Often, the mental illness itself prevents the shared intimacies that contribute to a marriage. Perhaps your spouse is very depressed and does not feel like talking. Some mental disabilities, such as schizophrenia, may interfere with a person's ability to concentrate or to tolerate closeness. In either case, the effect is to make you feel as if you are living with a stranger. The failure of the mentally ill to share in small talk can be especially disheartening. Said one person, "I can stand anything but his silence. He just sits there and doesn't say a word to me."

The emotional silence of your chronically mentally ill spouse means that you will be receiving fewer and fewer assurances that you are important and valuable. You are unlikely to hear that you look attractive, that supper was particularly tasty, or that you played a super game of volleyball. For each of us, feeling good about ourselves depends at least partly on feedback we get from our family. When this feedback is no longer forthcoming from your spouse, you may find that just as nothing you do seems to matter to him, it no longer matters to you, either.

In order to preserve your own self-esteem, you need a "thank you" now and again. Finding activities (such as hospital or church organizations, or families' groups) in which your contributions are acknowledged can remind you of your own value. This, in turn, helps to keep your energy level up.

You may need all the energy you can get, too, because in addition to talking less, your spouse may be doing less of his share of the work to keep things going. A previous arrangement for sharing household duties may no longer work. This can result in taking on more responsibilities yourself or simply letting some go. Taking over more and more of your spouse's previous contributions may produce anger and resentment. No matter how well you understand the mental illness, you cannot help feeling to various degrees that your spouse is not meeting his part of your marriage contract.

The feeling of anger may be particularly strong if you find that your spouse knew of his mental illness before marriage and kept this knowledge from you. Under these circumstances, the well spouse often feels betrayed and trapped and finds it hard to give needed emotional support. There is no easy way out of this dilemma, but it may help to remember that your spouse's secrecy was an understandable response to the shame unfortunately associated with mental illness. He was probably afraid of losing you, not deliberately attempting to "trick" you or cause you misery.

Financial insecurity can be a major source of difficulty for wives of chronically ill husbands. Many such women have never worked, others have stopped working after marriage, and some, though working, have been contributing only a small amount toward the family's income. Thus, the loss of your spouse's income because of chronic mental illness is a serious problem. Many spouses will have to return to work or find employment that pays more. In either case, they will take on the added responsibility of primary wage-earner in addition to the care of the spouse.

The upshot of all these losses—intimate confidant, coworker in the household, and income—is to undermine your sense of partnership in the marriage. In point of fact, you and your spouse will in many ways no longer be equals. The compromises and adjustments that the two of you had worked out will need to be reexamined and new ways of sharing devised. For example, one husband found that his wife no longer prepared meals following hospitalization. He discovered that while she was able to cook the meals with no trouble, she had great difficulty concentrating on the planning and shopping. She became confused and agitated about menu preparation. When he took over the planning aspects, leaving her a list of dishes to be prepared each day with food he had purchased, the problem receded.

Because chronic illness affects, in varying degrees, the ability to care for oneself, the healthy spouse will be forced to assume a parental role with respect to the other spouse. This may require you to make sure your spouse eats well or dresses properly. You may have to set limits for a spouse who cannot control himself. For example, a spouse who squanders money during episodes of elation or anxiety may have to be given a strict spending limit and restricted with respect to credit-card use. Your spouse may require you to structure his activities or to ensure that he does not simply pass the time completely inactive.

The assumption of a parental role by one spouse with respect to the other will be opposed by all interested parties. The ill spouse may well resent your "taking over." To argue with him that if you do not protect his interests, no one else will, is not convincing from his point of view. He will probably be feeling poorly about himself already. In his eyes, treating him "like a child" will be further evidence of his incompetence.

Social expectations also will be violated. There will be considerable pressure from family, friends, and professionals to give up your "parental" stance toward your spouse. Indeed, some will see your change in role as a contribution to the mental disability. Statements like "He'll never make anything of himself if you keep babying him" or "Don't treat her like a child" may confuse and distress you.

Finally, you yourself will resist this role. Years of psychological interdependence and counting on each other to share responsibilities will make it hard for you to give up or lower your expectations. You may think it is incorrect or inappropriate to take on parental functions. Nevertheless, you will often be forced by circumstances to do just those things, thus creating conflict between what you think you should do and what is actually required of you. Physically, emotionally, and psychologically, you will find yourself torn between the need to care for your spouse and your own need to depend on someone and be cared for.

In addition, others' embarrassment, your difficulties in explaining mental illness, and people's discomfort with mental illness make social encounters difficult. Frequently social invitations are given up or the well spouse begins to go out alone on occasion. It is far easier to provide an excuse for your ill spouse's absence than to explain socially inappropriate behavior or suffer embarrassment. People may indeed begin acting toward you as if you were a single person rather than a spouse. The more you avoid discussion of your ill spouse, the more people will respond to you as a single person.

Disruption of the usual sexual relationship between spouses often accompanies mental disability. This disruption is especially frequent during the early acute stages of the disorder. The way in which sexual relations are affected varies considerably. At one extreme is the very excited, manic person who suddenly "wants sex all the time." This sort of person is not only driven in his sexual arousal but can also become angry and hostile if frustrated.

Far more common is the spouse who becomes sullen, quiet, and withdrawn. Mental illness is usually associated with a decline or loss of interest in sex. For some, nothing is as pleasurable as it once was, sex included. For others, the intimacy and closeness that sex represents is so frightening that they withdraw. The well spouse often interprets this as a sign that he is no longer loved, important, or needed. Recall, however, that the ill person is probably responding to internal changes that are not directly related to others. It is unlikely that you have caused him to lose interest. It will help you to deal with your spouse if you interpret his sexual disinterest as a part of the mental illness rather than as a personal affront to you.

The change in the ill person's actions and attitudes may well cause the healthy spouse to feel as if something were wrong with his *own* sexual feelings. You might, on one hand, feel guilty for not having sex as often as your spouse would like, or you may feel that you are inappropriately "pushing" your spouse to have sex. Remember that the sudden changes in your spouse's sexual interests and drives are caused by his illness. You are neither "cold" nor "oversexed" for not keeping up with changes in your spouse's sexual desires.

The ill spouse is not the only one who can lose interest. There are many reasons why the healthy spouse would also experience a decrease in sexual interest in the ill person. The relationship has changed so that the healthy spouse becomes more of a parent toward the ill spouse. The extra responsibilities, worry, and work involved in the care of the chronically mentally ill are tiring. Depression and frustration over the circumstances in which you find yourself can dull your senses. Perhaps most difficult to accept is the fact that you simply do not find your spouse as appealing as before. Aside from a common tendency for all couples to lose the passion of earlier years, the ill spouse may do or say things that will hurt your feelings. He no longer contributes to the marital partnership as before. He may act strangely or be very distant. He may have become obese or sloppy. You are far better off in such situations to change the marital relationship so as to decrease or exclude sex than to fake emotions you no longer feel. Such an accommodation is frequently satisfactory to both partners and eases one source of pressure on them. Therefore, as it becomes clear that the ill spouse suffers chronic mental disability, many couples experience a serious reduction or elimination of intercourse.

Other couples find that their sexual relations vary considerably, largely depending upon the emotional state of the ill person. When the spouse can be emotionally close and is functioning well, sex is a natural part of the relationship. When, however, the spouse worsens or otherwise finds interpersonal relations straining, sex is avoided. Many husbands and wives have complained that they do not know from one week to the next (or from one day to the next) what sort of mood their spouses will be in—loving and close, or cool and distant. This unpredictability is emotionally draining and strains sexual relations over a long period of time. Some spouses seem able to adapt to this circumstance, while others cannot. The important thing is to work out, as best as possible, a relationship that satisfies both partners.

Sometimes, sexual difficulty occurs as a result of the medication used to treat mental illness. Certain of the antipsychotic medicines produce difficulty in sustaining an erection or impotence in some male patients. Therefore, if impotence does occur despite apparent sexual interest, a physician should be consulted. There is no clear evidence that medication produces changes in sexual desire in women, although sedative effects and unwanted weight gain may contribute indirectly to a decline in sexual interest in some cases.

A spouse's recovery can be just as traumatic for the marital relationship as the initial illness. One woman, for example, had given up sexual relations with her husband over the course of several years of his illness. They eventually found that affection and doing things together had replaced the physical and emotional intimacy of sex. Although she continued to have sexual desires, she tolerated the new relationship well. When her husband recovered and slowly began to reexperience his sexual urges, she was very ambivalent about her own feelings. She did not want to hurt him by not having sex with him, but he had become asexual in her eyes and it was very difficult for her to change this view. Most couples will not experience such a dramatic shift, but they will often face minor versions of this situation. As the spouse of a chronically mentally ill person, you must overcome both the inertia of your current adaptation and your natural tendency to feel like you are the one doing all the changing and compromising. Sometimes change is possible, other times not. In any of these situations, your own mental health must be considered as well as that of your spouse. In working out an arrangement that is best for you, it will help to remember that sex is but one part of an interpersonal relationship. Sex without affection can be just as impersonal and distant as no sex at all.

For those couples with children, chronic mental illness presents some difficulties in child rearing. First of all, a spouse may find himself functioning as a "single parent." As in any one-parent family, it is important to try to distribute daily responsibilities among the children. Outside help, child-care centers, or various structured programs can help ease some of the strain. Far too often, healthy parents find themselves becoming the sole source of support for the rest of the family, at the risk of their own well-being.

It is common and natural for the healthy spouse to feel an intense desire to have normal children to make up for the ill spouse. Such spouses will do as much as they can to protect their children from the disruption caused by mental illness. They gain much satisfaction from their children's accomplishments and their normal development. However, care must be taken not to isolate family members from each other or to put undue pressure on the children. Also, it is essential that you not completely give up discipline in the name of "trying to do everything" for your children.

Finally, there is always the difficult choice of whether or not to have children if you do not already have them. Is it a good idea? Can the couple cope with children? What are the chances that your children will also suffer from chronic mental illness? Can living around a chronically mentally ill person harm a child's development? Many of these questions can only be answered for individual circumstances. For example, the statistical risk for mental illness among children of a mentally ill person, while generally increased, varies with the type of disorder. There are other considerations in the decision to have children, including the ability of the ill spouse to share the responsibilities, your financial situation, and access to outside resources. Counseling can be especially helpful in the assessment of your own situation. Ultimately, however, the choice must be made by you and your spouse.

Facing all of these problems can be draining and disheartening. Nobody bargains for mental illness when he or she marries. Spouses frequently feel cheated and unfairly burdened. It is likely that the thought of separation or divorce enters the mind of each person with a mentally disabled spouse. Living with a stranger who drains your emotional and financial resources can be far worse than living with no one at all. Yet most people find the option of divorce both frightening and guilt-provoking.

You may feel that your spouse would be unable to take care of himself alone. You may be frightened, quite realistically, that he will need rehospitalization or that he will be hurt or abused. Your spouse may have threatened suicide or harm to you during discussions of separation. Particularly if he has been violent in the past, you may actually fear for your life or his and feel trapped by this fear in an empty marriage.

You may experience strong moral qualms about leaving someone who is sick and not responsible for the pain he has caused you. You may be angry at yourself for having "selfish" thoughts about "deserting" your spouse and might try to put them out of your mind. You may also have religious beliefs that preclude the possibility of divorce.

Family and friends may reinforce your guilt by expecting you to go on and on taking care of your spouse. Sometimes they do this out of worry that if you leave, they will be left with more responsibility than they would like. You may, in fact, agree that the burden of your spouse's care would fall upon your children, who have their own families and lives. You may not be able to "desert" *them* in this way.

Sometimes it happens that a spouse will become so used to being a caretaker and only a caretaker that he cannot envision losing this special role. It has become the only role he has.

As a result of these emotional, social, and religious forces, many people simply do not consider separation or divorce as an option. Those that do are virtually guaranteed a rocky, painful period of adjustment.

Divorce laws vary from state to state. In some, mental illness is itself grounds for divorce. Sometimes commitment is the criterion, while in other areas, the ill spouse must have been a psychiatric inpatient for a certain length of time. On the other end of the spectrum, some states will not allow you to sue a mentally ill person for divorce, no matter what the grounds. In those in which you can sue, some require that a guardian be appointed to protect your ill spouse's interests, while in others no guardian is necessary. Obviously, a competent divorce lawyer must be consulted as a first step in gathering information about your options.

If you have decided upon divorce and your spouse is in treatment, you should inform his therapist or treatment team of your plans. They can then make arrangements for whatever additional support, care, or protection may be necessary. Not only will this be helpful to your spouse, but it will also be one way in which you begin to transfer responsibility for the care of your spouse to other responsible people or agencies. If your spouse is not in treatment but is unable to care for himself, try calling the state agency that looks after mentally incompetent adults. It may be called the Department of Public Welfare, the Department of Social Services, or something similar, depending on the state in which you live.

In some states, you may be able to have a guardian appointed by the court to look after your spouse's financial interests and general welfare. You may want to seek the advice of an attorney about this.

If you believe yourself or your spouse to be in physical danger, seek advice both from mental health professionals and from an attorney. In these cases, as well as in those where the responsible spouse feels guilty about the new, less satisfactory living circumstances of his ill spouse, moving some distance away may facilitate the separation.

Parents

For parents of the chronically mentally ill, there can be no escape. A spouse may obtain a divorce. A sibling or child may concentrate on his own developing family and may even move far away. Although other relatives may carry a full measure of anger, guilt, or sorrow, parents are additionally burdened by the emotional and financial responsibility of caring for a child who may have never quite grown up. Further, unlike parents of a physically disabled child who receive the support, sympathy, and respect of friends, family, and professionals, parents of an emotionally disabled offspring may be ostracized and stigmatized.

Like other parents, the Laceys find that as they become older, they have less and less energy with which to cope with Steve's problems.

> BETTY: You know, I'm getting to the point where I really don't want to be bothered. I'm not at peace with myself.
>
> TOM: We've had it for nine years, you know. Truthfully, what we've been through, it's tougher now. It's bothering me more now.

This loss of energy is partly a result of the gradual loss of hope that parents experience as their child gets older but not radically better. The discrepancy between his age and his emotional maturity becomes greater and harder to handle over time. Not only is there disappointment and grief but increasing practical problems as well. For example, one parent related her concerns about her son's owning a hunting rifle. Despite the fact that he was twenty-two years old, she felt he could not be trusted to handle it appropriately. Since he had been violent when acutely ill, his mother was concerned lest he use the rifle to hurt someone. Nevertheless, he insisted that it was his and that he should be allowed to keep it. Similar concerns can arise about the person's competence to drive a car, take a trip, or get married. Parents do not want to baby their child, but they must try to protect him and others from harm. Frequently, there seems to be no satisfactory solution.

Naturally, parents wonder how the chronically impaired child will be cared for if they themselves should die or become disabled.

TOM: I worry about the future. Who will take care of him? We can't even leave him the house. He wouldn't be able to pay the upkeep. And they'd take away his disability money. It wouldn't even do him any good. How will he make it?

Tom is certainly right in thinking that an outright gift to Steve would soon be consumed by the agencies who provide him services. However, while legal provisions vary from state to state, there are two major strategies you can use to provide for your child after you die. The first involves making a simple will that *excludes* the impaired child. The assumption behind this plan is that whoever inherits the estate (usually one of your other children) has agreed to expend a fair portion of the assets for the benefit of the disturbed family member. In fact, a letter expressing that desire should accompany the will. In the Laceys' case, Tom and Betty could leave their house and savings to Sarah with the understanding that she would use it, as they had done, to provide Steve with "extras" that his Social Security disability checks could not cover. The positive feature is that government agencies can be relied upon to provide basic necessities and will be unable to take that money as reimbursement for services, since it does not belong to the mentally ill person. Further, the funds will be controlled by somebody who presumably knows and cares about the person and who can exert better judgment about how the money should be spent than could the ill member himself. This plan is particularly useful when the estate is small and cannot be expected to provide the person's necessities over his lifetime.

One of the drawbacks of this plan is that it may confer some tax disadvantages on the person who inherits the estate. In addition, it places that person in the parental role, with all its responsibilities and inconveniences. Further, the letter of intent may not be legally binding, so that you must have a great deal of trust in the person who is to inherit the money.

The second plan involves the creation of a trust fund intended specifically to *supplement* the ill person's earnings or governmental financial assistance. The success or failure of the trust instrument apparently depends on writing a very strong "spendthrift clause" and being lucky enough to live in a state in which such clauses are strongly enforced. A spendthrift clause states, essentially, that the trust money may not be used to pay any debts incurred by the beneficiary, but is to be used only for the purposes specified in the trust. Trustees (people who are named to manage the trust) can be specifically instructed *not* to use the trust to provide basic services, *not* to reimburse the government for providing such services. You can appoint the trustee, and you can be quite specific about the powers and duties of the trustee. You can even instruct the trustee to terminate the trust and give the money to someone else (for example, your other children) if there are legally enforceable claims for reimbursement that would defeat the purpose of the trust.

Obviously, the services of a knowledgeable attorney are indispensable. Since statutes and provisions are complex, subjectively interpretable, and vary from state to state, you would be well advised to try to find an expert who is experienced in providing for mentally disabled individuals. This is, of course, easier said than done. While most cities have a lawyer reference service, many of those services do not list specialties. A families' group or the Mental Health Association may know attorneys who can be helpful. If all else fails, try the state or local Association for Retarded Children. Since the issues are in many ways similar, a lawyer experienced in providing for the retarded will probably be able to offer sound advice.

Regardless of what plans are made, they should be understood by all family members. Someone should take responsibility for making necessary decisions about the ill member in the present, and contingency plans should be made for the future. One woman wrote into her will that a particular mental health professional had agreed to act as consultant to the family. She specified a wish that the family seek the advice of this professional when planning for her mentally ill daughter. If you have found a supportive professional who knows your relative, you may find such a stipulation helpful.

Parents should be aware of one other bit of legal information. Individuals who are disabled (physically, mentally, or emotionally) are entitled to a free appropriate public education. In most states, this covers individuals until the age of twenty-one. The local school district must provide or pay for appropriate educational services for your child, although again it will probably be up to you to advocate (and agitate) until the services are provided. Some localities have educational advocates who can help you, but you cannot expect the school to tell you where to find them. Try the state Department of Education or the Association for Retarded Children, which is used to fighting this particular battle.

Parents need not feel helpless about providing for their mentally ill children. Persistent, self-confident advocacy, while tiring and often frustrating, does result in dividends for the ill individual.

14

Growing Up
with Mental Illness

Brothers, sisters, and children of the chronically mentally ill experience anger, shame, guilt, resentment, and sadness at one time or another. Many of these feelings result from having grown up with a disturbed sibling or parent. Others are responses to current difficulties and living arrangements. Although siblings and children may more frequently escape the daily problems of chronic mental illness than spouses or parents, they often continue to suffer psychological and emotional consequences. In this chapter, we focus on these consequences, offering advice to parents on how to minimize them and guidance to young people about how to live with them.

A brother of a schizophrenic fears his being "mushy upstairs." Whenever this healthy brother is preoccupied or finds it difficult to concentrate, he wonders if this "is it." Is this his time to become ill? When will he become ill? Can he ever be sure?

The first in a long list of worries for parents and children alike is whether or not the well children will become sick. This worry has some basis in fact, since serious chronic mental illness does run in families. Close relatives of people who are affected are at increased risk of developing mental illness themselves. For example, while the rate of schizophrenia in the general population is 1 percent, the rate among first-degree relatives (parents, siblings, children) of a schizophrenic person is around 10 percent. Notice, however, that even though the rate is increased tenfold, *90 percent* of the first-degree relatives *do not* develop schizophrenia. Although the risk varies from illness to illness and from person to person, the same general conclusion is true for the various other illnesses: The great majority of even very close relatives are unaffected.

A related concern is whether your children (the grandchildren, nieces, or nephews of the disturbed individual) are or will be at risk. The statistical risk decreases as the biological relationship becomes more distant. Thus, if you are well, the risk to your children will be only slightly increased, if at all. The risk for second-degree relatives of a schizophrenic person, for example, is not significantly different from that of the rest of the population.

Far more serious is the *fear* that you will become or are ill. Perfectly normal periods of sadness, lack of concentration, desire to be alone, or lethargy are easily magnified in your mind as the first step on the road to mental illness.

Information, a counselor or therapist, family groups, and a sympathetic friend are all helpful in evaluating the seriousness of your "symptoms." While you do not want to underestimate mental illness, you should not allow normal behavior to take on disproportionate importance.

Secrecy

We are not yet able to predict or prevent mental illness, but the family can minimize the disruptive effects of the parent or sibling's illness on the well children. This does *not* mean that the children should be protected from contact with or deprived of information about their disturbed relative. On the contrary, an atmosphere of secrecy and shame is highly stressful for all family members.

The healthy children should be told all that they are capable of understanding about their relative's condition and should, on no account, be told a lie. This means, for example, that a mental hospital can be described as such to a teen-ager, or as a "hospital for people who are confused and unhappy" to a younger child, but should not be referred to as a "camp," "school," or "vacation." Teen-agers often profit from the knowledge of the name of their relative's illness, *if* they are educated about the proper meaning of the label by their parents, physician, or a thorough reading of pertinent literature. Younger children can be given a description of the major symptoms in language they can understand, as in the following example:

> Dad has a sickness that makes him very, very sad. That's why he sleeps so much and doesn't talk to us, and that's why he cries sometimes. It's not anybody's fault, it's just a sickness. Dr. Smith told us to take Dad to a hospital so she can try to make him feel better, and that's what we're going to do.

A straightforward explanation will not only help them in their interactions with their ill relative, but also will give them a foundation for coping with the social stress they will invariably experience as a result of the mental illness in the family.

The children should be encouraged to ask questions and to voice their fears. They will almost certainly want to know if the illness is "catching" (it is not) and what treatments their relative is receiving (pills, shots, talking to a doctor).

Children who want to visit their relative in the hospital should be allowed to do so if they are old enough to be accepted as visitors by the hospital. Usually, children are more tolerant of the odd behaviors they may observe in the other patients than are their parents. A child's comfort while visiting depends, in part, on the parents' maintaining a low-key, matter-of-fact attitude. If a child seems unduly distressed following a visit or does not want to return, it would be wise not to force the issue. In general, you can rely on your child's responses to guide your decisions about visiting.

Children may have silent questions, like whether their own thoughts or deeds are responsible for their parent's or sibling's illness. You will want to reassure them by both word and deed that they are not at fault. They will also want to know if their relative is going to die or get better. Again, a hopeful but realistic stance is best, as in the following example:

> The doctor says Dad will probably get a lot better than he is right now and won't feel so sad. But he may get very sad like this again from time to time.

Parents may not know the answers to all of the questions their children ask. It may be helpful to request that some member of the treatment team meet with whoever else in the family has questions and concerns (including, perhaps, the children, siblings, grandparents, and even aunts and uncles if they are involved with the disturbed individual), so that the parents do not have to carry the burden entirely alone. A meeting like this may help the family to work better together as a team and will aid in the flow of information among family members.

Frequently, it is helpful for the disturbed individual to be present so that he, too, will know what the family's concerns are. Even though some family members may be uncomfortable discussing the disturbed individual in his presence, doing so usually reduces tension. As an example, consider the family of a twenty-year-old woman who had made a serious suicide attempt. Her parents and eighteen-year-old brother, not wanting to "upset" her or "put ideas into her head," chose not to discuss with her their fears that she would do it again. Instead, they furtively arranged never to leave her alone. They could not help but resent the imposition on their freedom, and she could not help but feel stressed by their unspoken watchfulness. After being urged to do so by her therapist, they communicated their fears to her and were surprised and relieved to hear that she did not feel suicidal and was even prepared to alert them if she felt herself becoming depressed again. Apparently, she had not talked with them about her feelings because she had not thought they wanted to discuss it!

Disproportionate Attention

The siblings of chronically mentally ill individuals inevitably receive less attention than the ill sibling, particularly if the children are older and seem to need less parental attention.

Even before mental illness is recognized and officially diagnosed, the ill child's behavior often requires special attention from the parents, thus taking time away from the other children. Some chronically mentally ill adults were slow as children. Others were shy, abrasive, or demanding. Whatever the particular style or interpersonal relations of the child, it frequently placed extra demands on the parents' time. While all of the other children could be counted on to get ready for school, the ill sibling may have needed extra prodding. Perhaps mischief in school forced parents to be more involved with the ill child's teachers than with those of his siblings. Having a "sensitive" child easily hurt by criticism might have led the parents to go out of their way to accommodate family life to suit the ill child. Such an environment, from the viewpoint of the siblings, is one in which you are slighted, sometimes ignored, while your brother or sister often "gets his way."

A similar situation exists when a parent is mentally ill. The other parent may need to arrange for hospitalization, earn extra income, and attend to other matters, so that little time is left for the children. Most parents feel at times as if they just cannot fulfill everyone's needs. Visiting the hospital to see the ill parent, the healthy parent feels neglectful of his children. On a picnic with the children, the healthy parent is preoccupied with worries about the ill spouse. In short, siblings and children of the chronically mentally ill often resent what they perceive as being slighted by their parents.

Parents need not feel guilty every time those feelings are expressed. While the feelings are natural, they do not mean that the parent has behaved badly or is unloving. However, a certain amount of attention to and protection of the well children is advisable. Each young person in the family should be as free as possible to proceed with his own social and personal development. For example, an adolescent who is at dating age should not often be used as a "baby-sitter" for the disturbed family member. Nor should that young person be forced to include an ill sibling in his own activities. The important events in his life—award ceremonies, graduation exercises, sports competitions—should be attended by his parents whenever possible, even if this means foregoing a visit with the disturbed member from time to time.

It is not advisable to prevent healthy young people from going places or doing things solely because the ill child is unable to participate. For example, the Laceys were right to continue to allow Sarah to visit her grandparents even though Steve was uncontrollable and therefore unable to go. The general guideline is to allow each family member to accomplish whatever he or she is able to do.

Like the Laceys, most parents of mentally ill children feel the need to "make up to them" for the suffering they have endured. Betty says:

> I feel sorry for Sarah, too, but she has her husband and his family and friends. What does Stevie have besides us? Nothing.

However, it is important to resist filling this need by burdening the nonaffected children. They will need to have interactions with their parents that do not revolve around mutual worrying about the disturbed member. They will need to be protected somewhat from their parents' feelings of guilt or uncertainty. They will need to feel that they can continue to depend on their parents, that their parents have the strength to guide the family through the crises it faces.

Still, no matter how hard parents try to protect them, healthy siblings and children of the mentally ill are forced by their circumstances to assume more responsibility and to "grow up" quicker than their peers. They may take on some of the same functions as parents, such as baby-sitting, helping to keep house, cooking, and planning social activities. While all children take on these sorts of responsibilities as they grow up, the siblings and children of the mentally ill may do so at an earlier age and have the added burden of responsibility for an ill person.

Irrespective of parents' behavior, the well children are likely to feel shortchanged from time to time and must try to remember that their parents are doing the best they can in a difficult situation. Sometimes even the best of intentions can fail to produce a good result. In one family, for instance, the healthy child was asked to visit a friend whenever the mentally ill child was extremely upset. The healthy child finally shouted at them one day, "I'm sick and tired of being told to go to a friend's house until everything settles down with Paul. When will you think of me for a change?" Despite the fact that her parents *were* thinking of her, this young woman felt that she was the one doing all the compromising and that she was being unfairly treated.

A better course may have been to make options available and to let her choose among them. Her parents might have said:

I know it's hard for you to be around Paul. We'd love to have you home from college at Christmas, but if you'd rather stay at school or visit a friend, it's okay. We'll understand completely.

Keeping the family functioning despite the disruptive effects of mental illness is no easy task. Parents can focus on each family member as an individual, respecting the feelings of the well children and allowing for differences of opinion. Parents and children alike must expect rocky times. They will not always approve of each other's actions, nor will they always agree. However, an open, understanding, noncritical attitude can help to reduce the dismay and loneliness that each family member feels.

Social Difficulties

The strain among young people in the family is especially great before mental illness is recognized since the ill relative's behavior is perceived as intentional during this early period. One brother of a schizophrenic remembers that he always felt as if his brother would "take over" or go out of his way to "get" him as a child. In one vividly recalled incident, this person had found a toy in a field and brought it home. Several days later, his brother (who was eventually hospitalized for schizophrenia) showed the same toy to the family, announcing proudly that he had found it. At the time, the healthy brother could only see this behavior as willful lying. In fact, his brother probably thought that he *had* found it, an early sign of the thinking disorder in schizophrenia.

At other times, the ill brother was seen as taking jokes too far, trying to get away with things, and in many ways being hostile toward his siblings. Naturally, resentment and anger were frequently the outcome of this relationship among the children in the family. Even today, when the healthy brothers and sisters understand that much of the trouble they experienced was an early sign of their brother's mental illness, they feel some of the anger of their childhood. As one sibling put it, "Twenty years of feelings don't go away at the word 'schizophrenia.' "

Mentally ill parents are likewise seen as "bad" rather than as "ill" by growing children. One daughter recalls:

You definitely had to defend yourself. He was the enemy. It didn't occur to us that he was crazy. He was bad, he wasn't crazy. And we didn't think anything could change that.

In addition, when the mentally ill relative is a parent, the growing child is left not only unprotected but also actually menaced by one of the people charged with his care:

> My whole life was scripted in fear. You couldn't go home, because you didn't know what you'd find there, so there really wasn't any safe place. You were out there in the world, unprotected.

One of the most difficult tasks for grown siblings or children is to face their childhood history and try to separate old feelings from their current relationship to the ill family member.

The resentment of young people toward one who disrupts their lives often takes the form of angry withdrawal. It may appear as refusal to visit the hospitalized family member, pointedly ignoring the person, or purposeful, prolonged absences from home. Others are usually dismayed by this attitude and respond by asking the young people to "understand" and to "have patience." Neither patience nor understanding tend to be imparted to young people in large measure. These are qualities that accompany maturity. Should parents try to force the children to interact with the ill member? Probably this is unwise, since those interactions are likely to be painful for everyone. It is better to strike a bargain wherein the well young person can choose whether and when to interact with his disturbed relative in return for which he agrees that his part of the interaction will be as calm and supportive as he can manage. However, when the mentally ill family member is a parent, the other parent may feel that such a bargain is inappropriate and may decide to insist on certain contacts as a minimum—for example, having dinner together as a family.

How would partial or total ostracism by the well children affect the disturbed family member? To the extent that they are responding to inappropriate behavior, they are at least representing a realistic social attitude and may even be doing him some good. Even if they are responding solely to their own resentment, the result may be sad, but it will not be catastrophic. No one source of support is critical for any of us. What matters is that we get some support from somewhere.

Social stigma and the shame of having a "strange" family member also can present major problems to the young person. The ill sibling or parent's need for attention, his taking over, his bizarreness, or his unpredictability can all be frightening to children and adolescents.

Such a family member can affect the healthy member's social contacts as well. A mother talked of her healthy child:

> Where she suffered was either she didn't want to bring her friends here or her friends didn't want to come because of him [the ill brother] kind of taking over. I think they knew some of the incidents that have happened here and were afraid . . . They didn't want to come because they didn't know what would happen. . . . I think it was crudeness. When he is sick, his language changes, his personal appearance, his habits, they're all so gross. I remember two boys came to visit. He acted so grossly and they looked at each other, but I'm sitting there smiling and trying to pretend nothing was happening.

Having a relative who is socially deviant can be embarrassing at any age. Adolescence, however, is a particularly sensitive time during a person's life when peer conformity and acceptance are very important. It is natural, therefore, for adolescent relatives of a mentally ill person to lash out against the threat he presents to their social acceptance.

Once the healthy young people have left home, they encounter conflicts that are specific to their situation. Most experience a great deal of ambivalence about the need to live their own lives and their sense of responsibility to both their brothers and sisters, and their parents. Siblings, more than any other close relative of the chronically mentally ill, find it easy to move away from the problems created by their ill brothers and sisters. It is not unusual to find a brother or sister living in a distant city from that of the mentally ill sibling. Siblings, and often children as well, accomplish the same thing by breaking off contact with the ill relative that Sarah Lacey did. In many ways, these people build walls around themselves as protection against the hurt they have suffered in the past and their fear of trouble in the future. They say, in effect, "That's it, I've had enough. I must live my own life, and the only way to do that is to cut myself off from the situation." This sort of response is one way of ensuring reasonable peace in your own life, free from the unpredictable intrusions of your mentally ill relative.

Naturally, removing yourself from the family in this way carries its own risks. You will feel some guilt for not assuming your share of the responsibility for the burden others in your family now face alone. They may pressure you to show concern, to return, to "come and visit once in a while." You will, in other words, feel guilt "at a distance." Often people are surprised that they continue to feel guilt or shame after they have moved away. Such people had thought that by putting physical distance between themselves and their families, they could ensure emotional distance. This strategy, however, does not always work, as you can never completely erase your family and past experiences from your memories and emotions.

Sometimes people try to cope with mental illness by acting as though it never existed. Their ill brother, sister, or parent remains a secret to all outside the family. This way of handling mental illness has its own disadvantage: You feel as if you are never completely understood or a part of the group. There is always a part of your life that no one knows about. You never really know if you are fully accepted because you have withheld a very important part of your life from others. While there is no way to be sure how people will respond to your having a mentally ill relative, you will probably find them more supportive than you had expected. Divulging and explaining the illness in a matter-of-fact way to trusted friends usually results in considerable relief.

Ultimately you have to confront your natural reluctance to tell a prospective spouse about your mentally ill sibling or parent. When should you talk about it? Is the disclosure worth the risk of scaring the person off? What about children? How closely should your prospective spouse be involved with your family difficulties? The issue is not whether to tell or not, but rather when and how. No matter how far away or withdrawn from the family you may be, growing up with a mentally ill brother, sister, or parent is a part of you that must be shared. It continues to have some influence on your life, even if only in your emotions and thoughts. It is, in short, a part of you that both you and the person close to you must learn to accept.

At the other end of the spectrum, some young people attempt to take on a great deal of responsibility for the care of the ill relative. How much should the opinions of the well children (and other family members) affect decisions about the disturbed family member? Remember Betty Lacey's comment:

> I remember Sarah putting up such a ruckus! "How could you leave your son in that place?" I was really torn . . . I felt guilty.

The answer depends, of course, at least partly on the age of the children. If the children are adolescents or young adults and if the parents are able to carry the responsibility, it is usually best for the parents to make it clear that they will make whatever decisions are necessary. During a crisis, the family needs a more structured "chain-of-command" than is normally necessary. This means that parents, while possibly soliciting the opinions of other family members, must avoid diffusion of responsibility and the resultant uncertainty and anxiety.

Even families who normally make decisions by consensus may find that this process breaks down in a particular situation and that the family must delegate responsibility to one segment (usually the parent or parents). As the family ages, responsibility for decision-making may be shared by or shifted to an interested and committed sibling or child. The major consequence of this type of relationship is a feeling that your life has been constricted. The more you give your relative, the less you have left over for yourself. The more you feel encroached upon, the more you feel you have given up, the angrier and more resentful you will find yourself feeling about the situation.

It will not be easy to work out the arrangement that suits you best. Even as an adult, you may feel that you are still the one doing all the compromising. You may still become angry or feel resentment. As one person described it, "I still find it hard not to take my sister's behavior personally." It is unrealistic to expect that you will suddenly forget all the bad times and act as if nothing had happened, although some personal counseling may help sort out the issues. You can learn to focus on the present, on your achievements, pleasures, and goals. This will reduce the pressure on you and on your relative as well.

V

THINKING
ABOUT THE FUTURE

15

What Families Can Do

Throughout this book we have discussed the difficulties, uncertainties, and sorrows with which the families of the chronically mentally ill struggle. The concerns and responsibilities may at times seem so overwhelming that you are unable to think about anything else. While we are not discounting the fact that life can never be entirely normal for you, there are steps that you can take to ease significantly your pain and sense of futility. Here are some personal examples of how various families have reshaped their lives in order to live somewhat more peaceably with chronic mental illness.

Mrs. Tabor, a woman whose son had been ill for several years, wished to spend less of her time and energy simply caring for her son. She had a degree in accounting but had not worked in that field since her son's first hospitalization. He had been in and out of the hospital for six years and always came to live with his parents when he was released. Taking care of him required fixing his meals, doing his laundry, supervising his medication, and taking him to a day hospital program. Mrs. Tabor found that she had increasingly less time for herself and felt trapped by the demands of her son's illness.

After years of sacrifices to help her son, she realized that she needed to develop some interests that would help her focus her thoughts elsewhere. She decided to attend graduate school in public health and arranged for her son to learn how to use public transportation so that he could get himself to his day program. This not only gave her some free time to investigate the possibility of a career, but gave her son a sense of pride in his greater self-sufficiency. Although she was busier, she was still able to devote attention to her ill son and other members of her family. In addition, she felt a sense of satisfaction that had been missing from her life.

> I think just trying to have other interests . . . becoming involved in the field has been a great asset to me because I feel . . . I'm no longer the problem, I'm trying to help solve the problems.

Mrs. Richards, another mother of a chronically ill child, was frustrated over her daughter's lack of progress. She felt angry, disappointed, and tired. Some of the time she blamed her daughter, accusing her of laziness or uncooperativeness. At other times she blamed herself for not visiting her daughter often enough in the hospital or for simply not having the energy to provide better support. The guilt and anger became so intense that she was unable to visit her daughter or complete her daily household tasks. She isolated herself from her friends and other family members. At times she felt numb, while at other times she found herself yelling uncontrollably at her younger son for otherwise minor disagreements. On occasion she felt such despair that she thought about killing herself.

Finally, Mrs. Richards was encouraged by her daughter's therapist to seek counseling for herself. This counseling was neither intended to be a part of her daughter's therapy nor supposed to have a direct impact on her daughter's condition. This therapy was strictly for Mrs. Richards' benefit. She sought out a private practitioner not associated with the hospital where her daughter was being treated. Mrs. Richards initially discussed with the therapist her difficulty in coping with her daughter's illness. Gradually, however, therapy focused more on Mrs. Richards' feelings about herself, her divorce, which occurred some time ago, and her relationships with other family members. In some sessions her daughter's name was never even mentioned.

Mrs. Richards was not grossly disturbed and was not defined by her therapist as "mentally ill." She did need a noncritical and supportive atmosphere and the opportunity to air some of her feelings about her daughter. In this environment she felt no need to apologize for her anger or to hold back the tears that sometimes overwhelmed her. She was able to review the years of disappointment and struggle and have someone listen to her and understand her pain. While expressing her feelings in therapy did not change her daughter's condition, it did enable Mrs. Richards to stop blaming both herself and her daughter. Angry and hurt feelings continue to plague her from time to time, but she has learned to tolerate them. Mrs. Richards was also able to "mourn" her daughter, as we discussed in Chapter 3. She learned that her sorrow was normal and grew out of her lost hopes and expectations. She realized that her daughter might never have the career and family that she had anticipated.

In turning from her daughter to herself, Mrs. Richards began to look more directly at her own feelings of inadequacy and her sense of isolation. She had not worked since the birth of her first child, and life generally seemed empty and meaningless. She was divorced, her daughter was hospitalized, and her son was a rather independent adolescent. During the course of therapy she began to realize that with all of the problems that had occupied her attention in the past several years, she had grossly neglected her own interests. Her therapist helped Mrs. Richards formulate some short- and long-term goals for herself. Initially she joined her church's bridge club, an interest she had laid aside many years before. She met some new friends, whom she joined on shopping trips and movies. This introduction of leisure-time activities into her life gave her an enthusiasm that she had not felt in a long time. She began to attend church services more regularly and found that renewed religious conviction made her feel more fulfilled.

Very slowly she began to think about returning to work and using the business degree she had earned. Although her years out of the work force made her feel somewhat inept, she had several interviews and eventually obtained a job in a pharmaceutical company, where she has been working for the last six months. Mrs. Richards is now too busy to dwell continually on her daughter's situation. She has her daughter home on some weekends, and though these times are often difficult and unpredictable, she is not as devastated as she used to be when things did not go smoothly. She also feels freer to enjoy the good times with her daughter, since she is not as tormented by her own depression and anger.

Mrs. Richards no longer sees her therapist regularly but calls him from time to time when she feels the need for extra support or specific advice. Mrs. Richards' new perspective has helped her daughter, who is not as tense around her mother. She feels less guilt and pressure to live up to an image of a normal young adult. All this has not, however, significantly altered the course of her illness; she is still in therapy and continues to work toward further improvement.

Family Self-Help Groups

Many families have found solace and help in each other. Mr. and Mrs. Brighton had spent several years battling the mental health system in an effort to help their daughter, who had been diagnosed as having paranoid schizophrenia. They had been through several commitment hearings and multiple hospitalizations. They had dealt with countless professionals, many of whom seemed unaware of and even insensitive to their feelings. They were often confused about their daughter's illness, but did not know how to question the professionals, who always seemed so busy and aloof. They felt helpless and alone.

In the course of visiting their daughter in the hospital, they began to meet and talk with other families who were also frustrated, bewildered, and angry. Many of these family members seemed eager to talk and to share their pain with someone else who would understand. The Brightons decided to hold a meeting in their home for any family members who simply wanted to sit down and share their feelings and concerns. The first meeting produced an incredible outpouring of stories— poor experiences with professionals, frustrations with the mental health system, anger at mental health laws, pain and disappointment during years of dealing with mental illness. Many more similar meetings were held. Later they obtained some publicity from the local newspaper and elected officers. Within two years they had 150 dues-paying members. Mutual support, empathy, and emotional understanding have been an essential part of the group, as they note:

> we have a service that we can offer to families in giving them a crying towel, and it lets them let off steam, sort of an escape valve.
>
> They're uptight, bewildered, alone, forsaken by the world, battered by the law. They don't know where to go and they come here. People come out of here and . . . their shoulders come up, they straighten up again. Some of them are so . . . profusely thankful it's almost embarrassing.

Family members have learned in these meetings that they need not be the targets of blame or embarrassment. In order to offer emotional support, families' groups need have no great clinical expertise. In fact, families may more freely express their concerns without the presence of experts.

The group also provides an exchange of ideas and the distribution of information to its members. The varied experiences of the families are an excellent source of information about the mental health system and handling problem behaviors of their relatives. As families themselves become expert in procedures of commitment, financial assistance, consulting practitioners, and other aspects of chronic mental illness, they can share valuable ideas and successful strategies with less experienced family members. To augment the families' own experiences and information, the group holds meetings to which guest speakers are invited to discuss such subjects as violence, the mental health laws, and financial assistance. The professionals who are invited to speak are generally sympathetic to the families' plight and thereby do not undermine the function of the group. In fact, numerous professionals have referred their clients to the group for support.

In addition to the information meetings and the more informal talk sessions, the group has a telephone hot line. Members of the group are available as "counselors" to help families who require immediate help during a crisis or simply need to talk. They are also able to make referrals to appropriate agencies, lawyers, and practitioners. The telephone service has been an extremely popular and valuable aspect of the group in that family members can find comfort and information immediately when they need it rather than wait until a practitioner is free to return their call. As the group successfully meets the families' immediate needs, attention starts to turn to other tasks.

> We began to realize that there was more than just talking to each other about our problems. We had to think about doing something about them.

Thus the Brightons began to channel families' excess anger and frustration into constructive social and political action.

One of their aims is to educate the public about chronic mental illness and society's role in the care of the chronically ill. The fear and distrust that many people have of the mentally ill grow out of lack of knowledge and experience. As a result, they shy away from contact with the mentally ill. Therefore, the thrust of general education is to decrease fear and misunderstanding. It is hoped that such an educational program will result in a public more willing to vote for needed programs and in politicians sympathetic to the plight of the mentally ill.

Housing and finances represent a second major target for the family group's effort. Families and professionals alike feel that many more mentally ill individuals could make a satisfactory adjustment to the community if they had some semi-independent housing that would allow for self-sufficiency as well as offer supervision and support. There are halfway houses and transitional apartments. Both are designed with either live-in or on-call supervision and are meant for those individuals who do not need full-time hospital care but cannot manage completely independently. This type of facility, rare enough to begin with, is generally regarded as a transition between hospital and independent living for those who can go on to a place of their own at some foreseeable point in the future. There is almost no place in the community for those individuals who require some supervision for the rest of their lives but otherwise could function satisfactorily in the community. Obstacles to the development of housing for the mentally ill are great. Funds are lacking and public objection is high.

In addition to poor housing, the financial straits of the chronically mentally ill are severe. While we enumerated in Chapter 11 some of the agencies that can provide financial assistance, the total amount that they can provide offers only a very basic subsistence standard of living. Many of the chronically mentally ill have difficulty obtaining jobs due to the stigma attached to mental illness, their poor work history, and often their need for close supervision. Those who obtain jobs sometimes have trouble keeping them because of their residual symptoms or relapses. The lack of funds and of appropriate housing combine to create a poor quality of life for those individuals who attempt to adjust to community living. Many find the adjustment too strenuous and they return to the security of a hospital environment. In this milieu their physical needs are met and they are provided with leisure-time activities and friends.

Family groups have been working hard to make community living more attainable and desirable for their relatives. They have become advocates for the chronically mentally ill, especially trying to convince public officials that development of community facilities makes good economic sense. Legislators must be shown that provision for an individual in the hospital will cost more over the long run than provision of decent buildings, support personnel, and activities in the community. In many instances a careful review of the best ways to redistribute already available money is required. Another method is to initiate private funding and support. Often a private foundation, business, or religious institution can provide invaluable support and facilities for programming.

Finally, the Brightons' group has spent considerable energy in advocating for more humane and rational mental health laws to protect the individual's rights while also taking into consideration the family's and society's well-being. They have in fact been instrumental in some recent changes in their state's commitment laws, making the commitment process less formidable and more available when an individual requires treatment.

The Brightons' group has had both successes and difficulties in the pursuit of these goals. One of the major problems has been for the group to maintain its dual purposes of support and political action without spreading itself too thin.

Another difficulty has been inconsistent attendance by some family members. Once a crisis has passed, families no longer feel the acute need for support. They may even purposefully stay away from contact with other relatives of the mentally ill in order to try to have a brief respite from their problems. While this support aspect of the group is designed to help family members when they need the additional boost, the advocacy function of the group can work only through continued involvement and commitment.

In spite of these problems, the successes of the group have

been numerous. Nowhere else could families find the kind of empathy that is expressed by those who have been through the same ordeals. At present, the group is increasingly focusing on legislative change and advocacy. Some members are fighting for change in health insurance and Social Security regulations. Others are exploring funding for their own supervised housing program. The group continues to expand and gain recognition and has become a respected force in the mental health community.

For the Brightons the group has meant hard work and many hours on the telephone and meeting with others. However, their new-found self-confidence has significantly improved their relationship with professionals. Since they no longer feel inferior or defensive, they are more receptive to constructive collaboration.

Most of all the Brightons feel that they are doing something. They no longer feel helpless and swept along by their daughter's illness. They feel that they can have an impact on the future and that their lives are no longer solely concentrated on the illness.

We got the thing started and there are certain things we want done . . . I think this will be a way of life for the rest of our lives. Even if [she] gets well, fully well, fully recovered, I think there's a commitment there. And I think it's a sense of purpose and worth for our lives. Most of us lead selfish lives, we do what we want to do . . . and this is something where we can serve our fellow man, and on the selfish side, we'll have something to put on the good side of the Book when we get Upstairs.

If you have no such group available to you, you can start a family support group in your neighborhood with a minimal amount of organization and funds. If one or more families feel that such a group meets a need, they should first agree to hold a meeting and publicize it as widely as possible. The newspaper and the local mental health center are good places to start.

Meetings are generally held monthly and one of the first priorities should be the establishment of a telephone hot line. A newsletter is helpful to maintain interest among members as well as to provide information. Political action can be sustained by writing letters to elected representatives, attending local mental health association meetings and public hearings about mental health, speaking to local community institutions, and keeping the local newspaper informed of your activities.

Your group can receive assistance and information from a group established in 1979, the National Alliance for the Mentally Ill (1234 Massachusetts Ave., Washington, D.C. 20005). This association has essentially the same goals as smaller groups with emphasis on advocacy for the mentally ill and support and dissemination of information to the member groups. It seeks to improve community conditions, to provide information to the public, and to air families' needs and rights.

In contrast to widely held beliefs, families of the chronically mentally ill are not all evil, bad, or sick. For the most part, they are people who face an awesome task with fortitude, generosity, energy, and courage. Their ability to carry on in spite of the many obstacles is impressive and reminds us that chronic mental disability does not doom families to chronic defeat. Many gains have been made already. However, both as individuals and as a society, there is much to be done to ease your lives and to improve the future for you and your relative.

Family Self-Help Organizations

Arizona

Mental Health Advocates'
  Coalition of Arizona
1245 E. Concorda Dr.
Tempe, AZ   85282

Arkansas

Arkansas Parents of Adult
  Schizophrenics
c/o Park Hill Presbyterian
  Church
North Little Rock, AR
  72116

California

Advocates for Mentally Ill
Los Angeles County
17140 Burbank Blvd., Unit 107
Encino, CA   91316

American Schizophrenia
  Association
Alameda County
2401 LeConte Ave.
Berkeley, CA   94709

Association for Mentally Ill of
  Napa State Hospital
3438 Lodge Dr.
Belmont, CA   94002

Families and Friends of
  Mentally Ill
Stanislaus County
201 Stewart Rd.
Modesto, CA   95350

Families and Friends of
  Mentally Disabled
Santa Cruz County
315 Laguna St.
Santa Cruz, CA   95060

Families Group of Mental
  Health Association
Alameda County
1801 Adeline St.
Oakland, CA   94607

Families Group of Mental
  Health Association
Fresno County
1759 Fulton St.
Fresno, CA   93721

Families for Mental Recovery,
  Inc.
Humbolt County
P.O. Box 4404
Arcata, CA   95521

Families for Mental Recovery
Yolo County
718 Oeste Dr.
Davis, CA   95616

Marin Parents for Mental
 Recovery
Marin County
P.O. Box 501
Ross, CA   94957

Family Effort
2241 Rossmoor Dr.
Rancho Cordoba, CA
 95670

Parent Advocates for Mental
 Health
61 Morningsun
Mill Valley, CA   94941

Parents of Adult Mentally Ill
Santa Clara County
84 South 5th St.
San Jose, CA   95112

Parents of Adult
 Schizophrenics
San Diego County
5820 Yorkshire Ave.
LaMesa, CA   92041

Parents of Adult
 Schizophrenics
San Mateo County
P.O. Box 3333
San Mateo, CA   94403

Parents of Mentally Disabled
San Benito County
#24-1156 San Benito St.
Hollister, CA

Parents of Adult
 Schizophrenics
1740 Robinson, Suite 2
San Diego, CA   92103

Parents and Families of
 Schizophrenics
Napa County
P.O. Box 3494
Napa, CA   94558

Mt. Diablo Schizophrenia
 Association
Contra Costa County
2857 Patarmigan Dr., #2
Walnut Creek, CA   94595

Relatives and Friends Group of
 Metropolitan State Hospital
11400 Norwalk Blvd.
Norwalk, CA   90650

South Coast Schizophrenia
 Association
Orange County
2437 Winward Ln.
Newport Beach, CA   92660

Parents for Mental and
 Emotional Recovery
Contra Costa County
1149 Larch Ave.
Moraga, CA   94556

Friends and Families of
 Mentally Disabled
Riverside County
44981 Viejo
Hemet, CA   92343

Westside and Coastal Friends
363 20th St.
Santa Monica, CA   90402

Families and Friends of the
Mentally Ill
1740 Broadway
San Francisco, CA   94109

Foothill Families and Friends
for Mental Recovery
Auburn County
P.O. Box 234
Penryn, CA   95663

Colorado

Families and Friends of the
Mentally Ill
980 6th Street
Boulder, CO   80302

Support, Inc.
11335 West Exposition Ave.
Lakewood, CO   80226

Family and Friends of
Chronically Mentally Ill
4220 Grove St.
Denver, CO   80211

District of Columbia

National Alliance for the
Mentally Ill
1234 Massachusetts Ave.
Washington, D.C.   20005

Florida

Family and Friends Support
Group
M.H.A. of Palm Beach County
909 Fern St.
West Palm Spring, FL
33401

Parents of the Adult Mentally
Ill
666 Laconcia Circle
Lake Worth, FL   33460

Mental Health Association of
Palm Beach County, Inc.
909 Fern St.
West Palm Beach, FL
33401

Community Support Program
Human Resource Center
1220 Willis Ave.
Daytona Beach, FL   32014

Georgia

Alliance for the Mentally Ill
30 Chatauchee Crossing
Savannah, GA   31411

A.M.I.
Atlantic Chapter
3240 Lucile Ln.
East Point, GA   30344

Illinois

Schizophrenia Association of
West Suburban Chicago
P.O. Box 237
Downers Grove, IL   60515

Manic Depressive Association
P.O. Box 40
Glencoe, IL   60022

North Suburban Chapter
Illinois Schizophrenia
  Foundation
1510 East Fremont St.
Arlington Heights, IL
  60004

Concerned Argonne Scientists
Committee on Mental
  Dysfunction
Argonne National Lab.
Argonne, IL   60439

Illinois Alliance for the
  Mentally Ill
P.O. Box 1016
Evanston, IL   60201

Indiana

South Bend Family Support
  Group
403 E. Madison
South Bend, IN   46617

Parent Information Resource
  Center
1363 E. 38th St.
Indianapolis, IN   46205

Iowa

Iowa Schizophrenia Assn.
P.O. Box 334
Eagle Grove, IA   50533

North Iowa Transition Center
1907 S. Massachusetts
Mason City, IA   50401

Kansas

Families for Mental Health
4538 Meridan Rd.
Topeka, KS   66607

Kentucky

Society on Schizophrenia
511 Holmes St.
Terrace Park, KY   45174

Schizophrenia Association of
  Louisville
1816 Warrington Way
Louisville, KY   40222

Louisiana

A.R.C.E.D.
P.O. Box 511
Westwego, LA   70094

People's Alliance, MC.
1808 Edinburg St.
Baton Rouge, LA   70808

Friends of the Psychologically
  Handicapped of Greater
  New Orleans
P.O. Box 8283
New Orleans, LA   70182

Maryland

Threshold, Families and
  Friends of the Adult
  Mentally Ill, Inc.
3701 Saul Rd.
Kensington, MD   20795

Michigan

S.H.A.R.E.
2371 Valleywood Dr. S.E.
R. 11
Grand Rapids, MI   49506

Citizens for Better Care
163 Madison Ave.
Detroit, MI   48226

OASIS
1212 Parkdale
Lansing, MI   48910

Anawim
Loyola House
2599 Harvard Rd.
Berkeley, MI   48072

Relatives, Inc.
1562 Greencrest
East Lansing, MI   48823

Council of Mental Health
   Consumers
442 E. Front St.
Traverse City, MI   49684

Oasis Fellowship Inc.
Box 794
East Lansing, MI   48823

Minnesota

REACH
4141 Parklawn #105
Edina, MN   55435

Mental Health Advocates
   Coalition of Minnesota, Inc.
265 Fort Rd. (W. 7 St.)
St. Paul, MN   55102

Schizophrenia Assn. of
   Minnesota
6950 France Ave., Suite 215
Edina, MN   55435

Mississippi

Families and Friends of the
   Mentally Ill
Route 7, Box 500
Hattiesburg, MS   39401

Missouri

Alliance for Mentally Ill
14 S. Euclid
St. Louis, MO   63108

Huxley Institute for Biosocial
   Change
Kimler Building
10424 Lackland Rd.
St. Louis, MO   63114

Montana

North Central Montana
   Community Mental Health
   Center
Holiday Village
Great Falls, MT   59405

New Hampshire

Granite State Chapter
American Schizophrenia
   Association
Box 296
Meredith, NH   03252

New Hampshire Division of
Mental Health
Health & Welfare Building
Hazen Dr.
Concord, NH   03301

New Jersey

Concerned Citizens for
Chronic Psychiatric Adults
27 Prince St.
Elizabeth, NJ   07208

Mental Health Advocacy
Group, MC
340 12th Street
Palisades Park, NJ   07650

New York

Long Island Schizophrenia
Association
1691 Northern Blvd.
Manhasset, NY

Federation of Parents
Organizations
c/o Rockland Psychiatric
Center
Orangeburg, NY   10962

The Gateposts Foundation Inc.
P.O. Box 526
Bayside, NY   11361

Concerned Citizens for
Creedmore, Inc.
P.O. Box 42
Queens Village, NY   11427

North Dakota

Mrs. Hjordis Blanchfield
Rt. 1, Box 129
Devils Lake, ND   58301

Ohio

Community Services Planning
Project
222 E. Central Pkwy., 502-C
Cincinnati, OH   45202

Families in Touch
50 West Broad St.
Columbus, OH   43215

Oklahoma

R.E.A.C.H.
3113 N. Classen
Oklahoma City, OK   73118

Families in Touch
5 W. 22nd St.
Tulsa, OK   74114

Oregon

Taskforce for the Mentally and
Emotionally Disabled
718 W. Burnside, Rm 301
Portland, OR   97209

Save-a-Mind
411 Spyglass
Eugene, OR   79401

Parents for M.H.
1864 Fir South
Salem, OR   79302

Pennsylvania

Families Unite for Mental
Health Rights, Inc.
Box 126
Oreland, PA   19075

Main Line Mental Health
Group
108 E. Lancaster Ave.
Wayne, PA   19087

Families and Friends of
Morristown State Hospital
240 Roumfort Rd.
Philadelphia, PA   19119

Combined Parents for
Legislative Action
Committee, Inc.
Box 15230
Pittsburgh, PA   15230

Parents of Adult Mentally Ill
314 Birmingham
Pittsburgh, PA   15201

Families United of Oreland
P.A.
321 Sylvania Ave.
Glenside, PA   19038

National Society of Autistic
Children
Greater Pittsburgh Area
Chapter
414 Hazel Dr.
Monroville, PA   15146

Rhode Island

Project Reach-out
57 Hope St.
Providence, RI   02906

South Carolina

Families and Friends of the
Mentally Ill
P.O. Box 32084
Charleston, SC   29407

Tennessee

Mental Health Association of
Knox County
6712 Kingston Pike
W. Knoxville, TN   37919

Texas

The Huxley Institute for
Biosocial Research of
Texas/ASA
4415 Breakwood
Houston, TX

Virginia

Pathways to Independence
1911 Youngblood
McLean, VA   22101

Parents Group
1602 Gordon Ave.
Charlottesville, VA   22903

Schizophrenia Foundation of
  Virginia
Box 2342
Virginia Beach, VA   23452

Washington

Family Action for the Seriously
  Emotionally Disturbed
905 29th St., S.E.
Auburn, WA   98002

Community Family Group
9715 Fruitland Ave. E.
Puyallup, WA   98002

Schizophrenia Support Group
P.O. Box 5353
Vancouver, WA   98663

Advocates for the Mentally Ill
Box 5585
Seattle, WA   98105

Wisconsin

Alliance for the Mentally Ill of
  Greater Milwaukee
Box 16819
Milwaukee, WI   53216

Fox Valley Alliance for the
  Mentally Ill
1105 Canterbury Dr.
Oshkosh, WI   54901

AMI—Racine County
827 College Ave.
Racine, WI   53402

Alliance for the Mentally Ill,
  Dane County
R-8 1997 Hwy. PB
Verona, WI   53593

Alliance for the Mentally Ill
416 Windsor St.
Sun Prairie, WI   53590

Overseas Contacts

Australia

ARAFMI (Association of
  Relatives and Friends of the
  Mentally Ill)
Swanbourne Hospital
Davies Road
Claremont, W. Australia
  6010
Tel: 3841022

Victorian Schizophrenia
  Fellowship
1 Gwenda Avenue
Blackburn 3130, Victoria
Tel: 878 0710

New South Wales Association
for Mental Health
Suite 2, 1st Floor
194 Miller Street
North Sydney 2060
(also Branch of ARAFMI)

Austria

HPE ("Hilfe fur Psychisch.
Erkrante")
Spitalgasse 11/4 Stock
1090 Wien
Tel: 43 0755 or
65 72 99 (7:30–8:30 a.m.)

Canada

Ontario Friends of
Schizophrenics
Helen Lawson Building
327 Reynolds Street
Oakville, Ontario   L6J 3L5

Canadian Mental Health
Association, Manitoba
Division
330 Edmonton Street
Winnipeg, Manitoba R3B 2L2
Tel: (204) 942 3461

Association of Relatives and
Friends of the Mentally Ill,
Montreal, Que. Branch
5213 Earnscliffe Avenue
Montreal, Quebec   H3X 2P7

Society for Emotionally
Disturbed Children
1622 Sherbrooke West
Montreal   H3H 1C9

Japan

National Federation of
Families with the Mentally
Handicapped
1989-19 Oiso-machi
Naka-gun Kanagawa
Pref. Japan

New Zealand

Schizophrenia Fellowship
(N.Z.) Inc.
Box 593
Christchurch

West Germany

German Association of
Self-Help Groups
Friedrichstrasse 28
63 Giessen

Glossary

acute episode: a sudden severe flare-up of psychiatric symptoms.

advocacy: the attempt to protect or ensure the legal, economic, or moral rights of a person, particularly with reference to bureaucratic institutions (for example, the legal system, the social welfare system, the mental health system).

aftercare: services provided to a person following discharge from a hospital.

akathisia: a feeling of restlessness or agitation that may occur as a side effect of antipsychotic medication.

alcoholism: excessive, long-term drinking that ultimately impairs social or work relations. Symptoms such as shaking and hallucinations appear after sudden withdrawal of alcohol after chronic abuse.

anhedonia: diminished or lost ability to experience pleasure.

antidepressive: medication for the reduction of depression.

antipsychotic: medication to reduce disturbed thinking and to calm agitation.

anxiety disorders: any mental disability whose main characteristic is fear or apprehension, usually accompanied by autonomic system symptoms (such as dizziness, heart palpitations, or sweating).

behavioral contract: a formal arrangement in which someone agrees to modify his behavior in return for reward(s); the contract specifies the behaviors to be changed, how they are to be modified, and the conditions under which the rewards are given.

bipolar depression: a major affective illness marked by depression and mania, early onset, and increased family risk for psychosis.

breakdown: a term used popularly to describe serious emotional or mental disturbance; generally reflects major disruption of the individual's love, work, or play relations.

burnout: the gradual reduction of obvious psychiatric symptoms that occurs in some people who have been ill for a number of years.

case manager: a mental health professional responsible for the coordination of all services for a particular patient.

catchment area: a geographic area under the jurisdiction of a particular community mental health center.

childhood autism: a rare and serious mental illness which occurs in childhood and which is characterized by extreme social withdrawal and bizarre, stereotyped behavior.

correlation: a statistical measure that reflects the degree to which one thing changes as another does too; demonstration of a high correlation between two events does not prove that one causes the other.

day hospital: a program that may include therapy, recreational activities, and occupational training, for people who do not need the intensive supervision of inpatient treatment but who are not able to function in an unstructured setting.

deinstitutionalization: a movement intended to substitute community care of the chronically impaired for institutional care.

delusion: a false idea that is not correctable by reasoning or by the receipt of new information.

GLOSSARY

diagnostic label: a term used to refer to the dehumanizing aspects of formal diagnosis.

dystonia: a state of abnormal muscle tension that may be localized or generalized.

electroconvulsive therapy (ECT): a form of treatment, primarily for depression, in which electrical current is applied to the head so that a convulsion results.

euphoria: extreme good spirits; when used in a psychiatric context, it reflects inappropriate, uncontrolled affect.

first-degree relatives: relatives who share approximately half of their genes with the person in question, that is, parents, siblings and children.

hallucination: a perception, in any of the five senses, that has no basis in the external environment.

infantilization: the encouragement of dependency and childlike behavior in a person by treating him as if he were a child.

institutionalization: the placement of an individual in a hospital or some other residential setting for treatment; also refers to the changes (such as apathy, fear of the "outside") undergone by someone hospitalized for a long time.

major tranquilizer: the class name for a group of drugs used primarily in the treatment of psychosis.

manic-depressive illness: a serious disorder of affect in which depression and/or mania have occurred; "bipolar depression" currently is replacing this term.

mental disability: a term replacing "mental illness" that conveys the limitations in social, work, and play functioning imposed by long-term mental disorder.

minor tranquilizers: a group of drugs that are used to alleviate anxiety.

nervous breakdown: a popular term capturing the disruption in normal functioning caused by any form of emotional or cognitive disorder.

neurosis: though deleted from the most recent psychiatric classification system, a still commonly used term referring to functional disorders marked by ineffectual defense against or the presence of anxiety; "neurosis" generally implies less impairment, and more insight and contact with the environment, than "psychosis."

night hospital: the provision of lodging and evening supervision and therapy for people whose daily activities take place in the community.

occupational therapy: a method of treatment, by means of purposeful activity, designed to reestablish the capacity for industrial and social usefulness, to overcome disability, and to increase self-confidence.

paranoid: a thinking and interpersonal style marked by great suspiciousness, hostility and, in extreme form, delusions of persecution.

partial hospitalization: a program in which the individual spends part of each day in a hospital setting.

premorbid: the period of time before illness became evident.

prepsychotic symptoms: deviations from normalcy that precede the development of florid, overt psychotic symptoms.

prognosis: the estimation of the course, outcome, and duration of an illness.

psychosis: a group of mental disorders characterized by a gross loss of contact with reality and impairment in everyday functioning.

psychosocial: combinations of psychological and social factors that influence the development, treatment, and outcome of mental disorders.

psychotherapy: any form of treatment for mental illness or behavioral maladaptation that relies primarily on verbal communication between a trained person and a client.

psychotropic medication: drugs with an effect on feelings, thinking, or behavior.

recreational therapy: any free, voluntary, and expressive activity designed to enhance mental health.

relapse: a recurrence of symptoms in an individual who had previously recovered or improved.

remission: partial or complete abatement of symptoms or signs of a disorder.

residual symptoms: symptoms that remain after recovery from an acute psychotic episode.

schizophrenia: a functional disorder in which the person shows thought disorder, social withdrawal, and either inappropriate or blunted affect.

second-degree relatives: relatives who share, on the average, a quarter of their genes in common with the person in question, that is, grandparents, grandchildren, aunts, uncles, nieces, and nephews.

sheltered workshop: a structured, supervised work setting in which patients engage in factory-type work, usually for reduced wages.

spendthrift clause: a statement in a trust instrument that disallows the use of the trust to pay the debts of the person for whom it was created.

stress: either psychological or physical strain.

tardive dyskinesia: a side effect, possibly irreversible, of long-term antipsychotic drug use; involuntary movement usually expressing itself as lip-smacking or tongue-thrusting.

thought disorder: the haphazard, illogical, confused, incorrect, or bizarre thinking that characterizes the psychotic state.

unipolar depression: major affective disorder in which a person experiences only depression. In contrast to bipolar depression, unipolar depression has a later onset and lower family risk for psychosis.

vocational therapy: treatment designed to train or retrain an individual for gainful employment.

Index

INDEX

expectations *(cont.)*
  for mental health professionals, 37–38
  patient, 93, 99–101

family
  as cause of mental illness, 52–56, 71, 78, 156–57, 161–62, 170
  conflict of, 70–74
  confusion of, 25–26
  counseling for, 162, 198–99, 202
  depression in, 33–34
  division of, 76–77
  expectations of, 43, 44, 70–73, 99–108, 111–13, 115–19, 122, 168–76
  extended, support of, 65, 79
  fear in, 32, 126, 189–90
  guilt of, 7, 8, 10, 25, 28, 37, 49–58, 60, 62, 68, 122, 146, 175, 191
  hopelessness of, 44–45
  hospitalization and, 158–61
  isolation of, 7–8, 9, 43, 56, 73, 75–80, 199
  prognosis and, 34–35
  resentment of, 76, 168, 193
  resources for, 139–40, 152, 179
    books, 27, 68, 148
    support groups, 69, 147, 200–15
  shame of, 25, 28, 77–80, 113, 118–19, 126–27, 183, 190
  stress symptoms of, 53, 74–77
  therapy for, 29, 64, 139, 161–62
fantasy, 91, 93, 100, 112
fatigue, 134–35
fear
  in family, 32, 126, 189–90
  of leaving hospital, 41–42
finances, 203–4
  financial aid, 149–51, 152
  illness of spouse and, 169
  management of, 138, 144, 150, 205
  wills/trusts and, 178–80
food stamps, 151

Freud, Sigmund, 52–53
frustration, 37, 119

genes, mental illness and, 52–53
giggling, 118
goal-setting, 99–101
  behavioral contracts, 102–5, 108, 112, 114–15
grandiosity, 23, 115
guardians, legal
  for spouse, 176
guilt
  effects of, 57–58
  family, 7, 8, 10, 25, 28, 37, 49–58, 191
    anger and, 60, 62, 68, 175
    hospitalization and, 86–87, 146
    resentment and, 122
  patient, 200
  relief for, 58
  sources of, 52–56

hallucinations, 115–19, 128
  suicide and, 129
Harper, Robert A., 68
home treatment, 95–108, 149, 157–61
hopelessness, 44–45, 128
hospitals and hospitalization, 13–14, 17, 24, 144–47
  children's visits to, 183–84
  chronic illness and, 30–31
  commitment procedures, 145–47
  day hospitals, 97–98, 139, 147–48, 161
  dependency and, 40–41, 97
  fear of leaving, 41–42
  impact on family, 158–61
  lack of motivation and, 113–15, 119
  length of stay, 39–42
  night hospitals, 148
  outpatient services, 147–49, 152
  outside activities and, 41–42
  relapses and, 39
  remission and, 98–99
  state hospitals, 149–50, 152

INDEX

About the Authors

KAYLA F. BERNHEIM received a Ph.D. in clinical psychology from the University of Pennsylvania. She has taught at the University of Pennsylvania, Swarthmore College, and the State University of New York at Geneseo. She has worked as a staff psychologist at a State Mental Hospital and as clinical director of an adolescent treatment center. She is presently the consulting psychologist to the Livingston County Mental Health Clinic, New York.

RICHARD R. J. LEWINE received his Ph.D. from the University of Pennsylvania. He was recipient of a National Institute of Mental Health postdoctoral fellowship in longitudinal schizophrenia research. He has been professor of psychology at both the University of Denver and the University of Illinois at Urbana–Champaign. He is currently conducting research and teaching at the Illinois State Psychiatric Institute and the University of Chicago Pritzker School of Medicine.

CAROLINE T. BEALE, A.C.S.W., received her master's degree in social work from the University of Illinois, Chicago Circle. She worked for seven years as a clinical social worker and administrator at Norristown State Hospital in Pennsylvania. At present she is a private consultant in the Philadelphia area.